VOICES
FROM
UNOCCUPIED CHINA

By

LIU NAI-CHEN · TSAI CHIAO

C. K. CHU · J. HENG LIU · FEI HSIAO-T'UNG

WU CHING-CHAO · CHIN YUEH-LIN

EDITED BY HARLEY FARNSWORTH MacNAIR

THE UNIVERSITY OF CHICAGO PRESS

CHICAGO · ILLINOIS

THE UNIVERSITY OF CHICAGO PRESS · CHICAGO

Agent: THE CAMBRIDGE UNIVERSITY PRESS · LONDON · ENGLAND

[LECTURES ON THE HARRIS FOUNDATION 1943]

THE Harris Foundation Lectures at the University of Chicago have been made possible through the generosity of the heirs of Norman Wait Harris and Emma Gale Harris, who donated to the University a fund to be known as "The Norman Wait Harris Memorial Foundation" on January 27, 1923. The letter of gift contains the following statement:

It is apparent that a knowledge of world-affairs was never of more importance to Americans than today. The spirit of distrust which pervades the Old World is not without its effect upon our own country. How to combat this disintegrating tendency is a problem worthy of the most serious thought. Perhaps one of the best methods is the promotion of a better understanding of other nations through wisely directed educational effort.

The purpose of the foundation shall be the promotion of a better understanding on the part of American citizens of the other peoples of the world, thus establishing a basis for improved international relations and a more enlightened world-order. The aim shall always be to give accurate information, not to propagate opinion.

Annual Institutes have been held at the University of Chicago since the summer of 1924. The lectures delivered each year have been published in essentially their original form in a series of volumes of which this is the most recent.

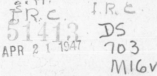

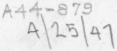

INTRODUCTION

SYNTHESIS OUT OF ANALYSIS: FOR REVIEWERS RATHER THAN READERS

STUDENTS of the Far Eastern scene, precontemporary and contemporary, and prophets of the post-war era will find this work—the 1943 annual volume of the Harris Foundation of the University of Chicago—of value, not alone for what its authors say, but for what they have left unsaid. The addresses herein contained are, in one sense, diplomatic documents, and diplomatic documents, as should be well known, bear reading between the lines. Often they are as notable for what they omit, or imply, as for what they boldly, or subtly, state.

I

Two decades ago, in 1923, certain funds were presented to the University of Chicago for the purpose of developing a segment of the American mind along international lines. The thought which lay back of this gift may have been that, no matter how charming the idea of perennially carefree youth seems when a Barrie creates a Peter Pan, the thought of a people essaying in world relations the role of "the boy who never grew up" is lacking in appeal. It may also have been feared that those fortunate ones who live in the Middle West far from the uneasy tides of ocean might more easily forget than others nearer the sea the fact that man does not live in a vacuum. In any case, those who have attended the nineteen annual institutes administered by the faculty Committee on the Norman Wait Harris Memorial Foundation of the University of Chicago have enjoyed the opportunity of discussing topics and problems related to many fields of thought: geographical, functional, and institutional.

Differing in detail from year to year, the method ordinarily followed has been that of inviting several authorities to deliver public lectures and to act as leaders in round-table discussions participated in by a group of invited guests intelligently interested in the topics under consideration. The volumes hitherto published by the Foundation have included the lectures addressed to the public. Planographed records of the round-table discussions have been available to the participants, and to a few others only.

In 1943 established custom was, in general, followed, but in detail there were several departures therefrom. First, it was decided not to consider topics related to a wide geographical field, such as Latin America or the Far East, but to concentrate attention upon limited parts of one country only—namely, Unoccupied China; second, to approach the topics chosen from one standpoint basically, namely, that of the National Government and the one legally recognized party, the Kuomintang; third, to hold a shorter conference than usual, with a smaller number of discussions, a more limited list of guests (about fifty), and without public lectures. In other words, the 1943 Harris Institute was a small, nonpublic, and, from the viewpoint of materials discussed, a one-sided affair—one-sided in that no attempt was made to deal with conditions and problems related to those very considerable areas of the country and masses of population not at present controlled by the government of Unoccupied China—which government, in turn, is controlled by certain committee members of the Kuomintang.

The determining factor for the indicated departures from custom in 1943 was the arrival, for one year, in the United States of a group of scholars, chosen, one each, by their respective institutions, with the official consent of the Chungking government for their departure from China, on invitation, not on nomination, of the Division of Cultural Relations of the Department of State of the United States government. The scholars are not official Chinese government representatives. Their object is to contribute to closer relations between Chinese and American educational institutions. The following excerpts from Press Release No. 239 (June 8, 1943) of the Department of State make clear something of the background of four of the leaders in the Nineteenth Annual Harris Institute.

[Several] distinguished Chinese professors left Chungking on June 5th to come to the United States for a year at the invitation of the Department of State. Their trip has been arranged by the Department in connection with its program of cultural relations with China.

The . . . . professors are:

Professor Yueh-lin Chin, philosopher, National Southwest Associated University; . . . .

Professor Hsiao-t'ung Fei, sociologist, National Yunnan University; . . . .

Professor Nai-chen Liu, political scientist, National Wuhan University; . . . .

Professor Chiao Tsai, physiologist, National Central University; . . . .

VOICES FROM UNOCCUPIED CHINA

Professor Chin has studied in this country and in England and speaks and writes English with great facility. He has published articles on logic in American and British journals. Professor Fei, although a young man, has already published, in English, a well-known book, *Peasant Life in China*. Professor Liu studied at the London School of Economics and Political Science and in leading European universities. He has written many books in Chinese on his specialty, local government. Professor Tsai is the leading research physiologist in China. He held a Rockefeller Fellowship for study in England in 1930–31. He is head of the Department[s] of Physiology [and Pharmacology, Medical College] at his university which has actively continued laboratory investigations and the publication of results throughout the war period. . . . .

During their stay of approximately one year in this country, these men will study recent work in their fields of learning, will travel and give occasional lectures, and will at all times endeavor to build up closer relationships between American universities and their own institutions in China.

In addition to the four gentlemen listed above in the press release, three others—including two medical doctors, J. Heng Liu and C. K. Chu, and a sociologist, Dr. Ching-chao Wu—in the employ of the (Chungking) National Government of China were invited to participate.

II

Five round-table conferences were held—the first four in the Public Administration Clearing House, the last in the Shoreland Hotel—on Thursday (morning and evening), August 5; Friday (morning and evening), August 6; and Saturday (morning), August 7. The topics discussed, the discussion leaders, and the University faculty men who chaired the conferences, were, in sequence:

Government and politics—Professor Nai-chen Liu; chairman, H. F. MacNair

SYNTHESIS OUT OF ANALYSIS

Public health—(1) "Problems of Nutrition in Present-Day China,"
Professor Chiao Tsai; (2) "The Modern Public Health Movement
in China," Dr. C. K. Chu; (3) "The Origin and Development of
Public Health Service in China," Dr. J. Heng Liu; chairman,
P. C. Hodges
Economic problems—Professor Ching-chao Wu; chairman, D. H.
Leavens
Social problems—Professor Hsiao-t'ung Fei; chairman, W. F. Og-
burn
Education—Professor Yueh-lin Chin; chairman, S. Y. Teng

Since it was not practicable this year to arrange for
public lectures, it was intended, prior to the opening of
the Institute, to forego publication of the annual volume and merely to distribute to the guests, in due
course, planographed reports of the round-table discussions. Nevertheless, to insure that nothing in the
nature of a Barmecide feast should ensue, suggestion
was made to the guests-from-afar, whose services had
been solicited as discussion leaders, that short papers be
prepared for presentation at the opening of each session.
With, possibly, two exceptions, this suggestion was
acted upon. The papers and informal addresses, which
served as bases for discussion, proved of such uniform
excellence in content and timeliness as to make it indis-
putably wasteful to embalm them in but a few-score
planographed copies of conference reports. Accordingly, the Harris Foundation Committee, in not too solemn
conclave assembled, decided that they should be edited
for publication in book form. This has been done with
the consent and aid of the seven characters who turned
into authors and, in the case of the papers and address
presented at the round table on public health, with the
greatly appreciated aid of Dr. Paul Hodges, who checked
the statements of his contributors for accuracy of

statement, scientific fact, and terminology in a field distinctly outside the competence of the volume's general editor.

Essentially, but not necessarily in word-for-word order, the papers and addresses hereinafter presented remain as they were offered. In the two cases where the informal, vocative style was adopted, that style has not been edited away, it being felt that the whimsical humor of manner and phraseology added to, rather than detracted from, the serious content of the messages delivered. No hesitation has been felt in attempting, on occasion, to correct unfortunate choices, or even errors, in grammar, style, and content. In a few places statements in reply to questions asked, following the delivery of the addresses and general observations by the authors, have been transferred from the journal record and inserted into their papers—or transformed into those polite embellishments, and buttresses, of scholarship known as footnotes.

III

The greater the amount of biographical knowledge in the minds of an author's readers, the greater the degree of illumination with which the readers will master that author's writings. Hence the attempt below (to paraphrase the words of a popular novelist) to give enough concerning the lives of this book's authors to explain their reputations. And, as playbills sometimes say, "Names of characters are given in the order of their appearance," at the conference.

Professor Nai-chen Liu (b. 1902) is a native of Anhui Province, in east-central China. An outstanding teacher and writer in the field of political science, he is making

his first visit to the United States. After attending
Wuhu Academy and the University of Nanking, both
American missionary institutions, the one in Anhui, the
other in Kiangsu, Mr. Liu studied in the University of
London for three years, upon completion of which study
he received the degree of Doctor of Philosophy. He
then entered into advanced research for two years in
Germany, chiefly in the field of municipal administration, in the University of Berlin and the Institute of
Municipal Administration. From the latter he received
a diploma and proceeded to the University of Paris, in
which he spent another year. For the last eleven years
he has been professor of political science and, during the
last six years, department head in the National Wu-Han
University, which institution, prior to the fall of Hankow to the Japanese in 1938, was located in Wuchang,
on the right bank of the Yangtze, across from Hankow
and Hanyang. In addition to numerous articles and
pamphlets, Professor Liu has written seven volumes in
Chinese, viz., *Comparative Government*, Volumes I and
II; *Municipal Government and Administration; Political
Reconstruction and the Spirit of Law; Theory and Practice of the New District Code; Local Government in Great
Britain; Local Government in the United States*.

Professor Chiao Tsai was born in China in 1898, a
year of intellectual and political ferment, which may
have influenced him in his global pursuits of knowledge.
In 1917–18 he was a student of Fuhtan College (later
University), a private, nonmissionary, Chinese institution in Shanghai. In 1918–19 he studied in the National
University of Peking. In 1919–21 he attended the Uni-

versity of California. In 1921-22 he paused for a year at Indiana University and received a Bachelor of Arts degree. During the following three years he studied in the University of Chicago, which, in 1924, made him a Doctor of Philosophy.

Upon returning to his native land in 1925, Dr. Tsai served for two years as professor of physiology in Fuhtan, and from 1927 to 1930 as an assistant professor of physiology in the College of Medicine in the National Central University, in Shanghai. From September 26, 1930, to December 25, 1931, he held a Rockefeller Foundation fellowship, during a year of which period he pursued studies, with distinguished success, under Professor C. Lovatt Evans in the department of physiology of University College, London. Then, after visiting physiology laboratories in England and Scotland, he worked for several months in Professor G. Embden's laboratory at Frankfort, Germany. On the expiration of his fellowship, Dr. Tsai returned to China (by way of the United States, where again he visited various centers of learning) to associate himself (1932-39) with the Lester Institute for Medical Research in Shanghai. In 1937 he became professor of physiology and head of the department in the Medical College of the National Central University at Nanking, a position which he held until 1942, when he accepted a government appointment as professor of physiology and head of the departments of physiology and pharmacology in the same institution. The ranking individual in his field, he has succeeded during the war years in carrying on in Chengtu, Szechuan—Four Rivers—Province, his direction of various laboratory researches with a minimum of equipment and has contributed greatly to the solution (or as great a degree of solution as is possible under existing conditions) of problems related to wartime nutrition and public health. Particularly has he co-operated in committee work along these lines connected with his country's armed forces. As Professor Tsai's publications in learned and professional periodicals number some two and a half score, limitations of space forbid their enumeration.

Dr. C. K. Chu (b. 1901) is a native of Chekiang, the province immediately to the south of Kiangsu, which is noted for its beautiful scenes of monastery-dotted mountains, swift rivers, Hangchow on the West Lake, the Hangchow tidal bore, and an island-fringed coast. A holder of degrees in medicine (M.D., P'eiping Union Medical College, 1929), and public health (Dr. P.H., Yale University, 1933), and a Fellow of the American Public Health Association (1943), Dr. Chu has filled a number of increasingly important posts during the last fourteen years. In 1929 he was physician-in-charge, School Health Service, P'eiping Health Demonstration Station. During the years 1929 and 1930 he served as chief of the School Health Service and director of the Kaochiao Rural Health Demonstration Station in the Department of Health, Municipality of Greater Shanghai. In 1930–31 he became director, First Health Demonstration Station, Department of Public Health, Municipality of Nanking. From the latter year until 1939 he was chief of the Department of Health Education in the Ministry of Health and the Central Field Health Station, during three years (1935–38) of which period he was executive secretary of the Commission on

Medical Education in the Ministry of Education. During 1939–41 he was director of the Public Health Personnel Training Institute of the National Health Administration, following which he became vice-director (1941–42) of the National Institute of Health in the same administration. In the spring of 1943 he was sent to the United States to serve, in May, as a delegate to the United Nations Conference on Food and Agriculture—consequent upon which he was invited to participate with Dr. Tsai and Dr. Liu in the Harris Institute round table on public health.

Dr. J. Heng Liu (b. 1890) is a native of Tientsin. He was graduated in 1909 from the Harvard Medical School in Shanghai with the Bachelor of Science degree and with the Doctorate in medicine in 1913. After holding a professorship in surgery in that school, he transferred to the (Rockefeller) Peking Union Medical College as associate professor of surgery. Soon he was appointed superintendent of the hospital (1923) and later (1930) director. Dr. Liu retired from the Peking Union Medical College to Nanking to become, first, vice-minister, then the first minister of health in the National Government following the setting-up of that government in the year 1928. In logical sequence he became, with the passage of time, director-general of National Health Administration in 1930, director of the Central Field Health Station, surgeon-general in the Army Medical Administration, present head of the Department of Medical Supplies of China Defense Supplies, Inc., in Washington, D.C., and a delegate to the above-mentioned United Nations Conference on Food and Agriculture.

Dr. Ching-chao Wu was born in Anhui Province in 1901. In 1916 he entered the then Tsinghua College, an institution, built with American-returned Boxer indemnity funds, in the park of an old Manchu palace a few miles to the west of Peking. This institution for several years devoted its energies in the main to the preparation of students for entrance into American colleges and universities. Later it gave less attention to preparatory work for those going abroad and gradually developed into a university outstanding in the Chinese educational system. In Tsinghua, Dr. Wu spent seven years before leaving to study at the University of Minnesota and the University of Chicago, the first of which, in 1925, granted him a Bachelor of Arts degree, while the latter conferred on him the two higher degrees in 1926 and 1928, respectively. During the following seven years Dr. Wu served as professor of sociology in the University of Nanking (1928–31) and the (by this time) National Tsinghua University (1931–35). From 1935 to 1937 he was senior secretary in the Executive Yüan of the National Government under the Five Power Constitution. Since 1938 he has been senior secretary in the Ministry of Economic Affairs. In April, 1943, he arrived again in the United States, having been sent by the government this time to study post-war problems with relation to China.

Dr. Hsiao-t'ung Fei and Dr. C. C. Wu co-operated in the leadership of the round tables dealing, respectively, with economic and with social problems. Dr. Fei (b. 1910) is a native of the province of Kiangsu, which, bordering Anhui on the east, is the last province through which the Yangtze flows into the Eastern Sea. Dr. Fei has recently served as acting head of the department of sociology in National Yünnan University and as director of the Yenching-Yünnan Station of Sociological Research. After beginning his collegiate career in (the American Methodist) Soochow University, in Soochow, Kiangsu, he transferred to Yenching University, another well-known American Christian institution, which, in times of peace, neighbors Tsinghua University and the old Manchu summer palaces at the edge of the Western Hills. In 1933 Mr. Fei received a Bachelor's degree, after which he entered upon studies, under the direction of the late Professor B. Malinowski, in the London School of Economics and Political Science, University of London. Here, in 1938, he received a Doctor's degree in social anthropology. On returning to his homeland, more than a year after the outbreak of Sino-Japanese hostilities, Dr. Fei entered upon a research program in rural economy as affected by wartime social and cultural conditions. Under a co-operative arrangement between Yenching and Yünnan universities, he directed, with the assistance of other specialists, a detailed survey of a small village in Yünnan. To the Mont Tremblant, Quebec, International Conference of the Institute of Pacific Relations, a preliminary report concerning these researches was made in December, 1942. Professor Fei's *Peasant Life in China*, a detailed analysis of conditions in a village a few miles from the city of Soochow, in his native province, Kiangsu, has been published by Routledge in London and Dutton in New York. Dr. Fei is also co-author (with two other sociologists, Yu-i Li of Yenching University and Tse-i Chang of Tsinghua University) and editor of a valuable monograph entitled *Three Types of Rural Economy in Yünnan*, published in 1943 by the Institute of Pacific Relations in New York, in which organization he holds a research fellowship.

Professor Yueh-lin Chin (b. 1895) is a native of Hunan Province in mid-China. A learned and, withal, delightfully wise product of the ancient classical educational system of his own country, as well as of the modern and somewhat more scientific American system, he is especially qualified to analyze China's educational and other cultural problems. He holds degrees from the University of Pennsylvania (B.S., 1917) and Columbia University (M.A., 1918; Ph.D., 1920), besides which he has resided for several years (1920–25) in England and on the European continent. Since 1926 he has been professor of logic and epistemology—to which fields he has contributed several publications—in Tsinghua University. As a result of the continuation of Sino-Japanese hostilities since 1937, this institution is now a unit of National Southwest Associated University in Kunming, capital of Yünnan, the province "South of the Clouds" (of Szechuan).

IV

And now, having placed in time and space and circumstance the nineteenth Harris Institute and its round tables, there remain to be made comments on the essay-addresses (and the ensuing discussions) which form the body of this volume.

In presenting for consideration a few of the innumerable and highly complex problems connected with contemporary Chinese government and politics, Professor N. C. Liu's task was, as a Chinese might phrase it, a little not light. Not only are the problems difficult of brief analysis before a non-Chinese group (most of the members of which had no firsthand knowledge of the country under discussion), but various of the issues are dangerous for Chinese citizens to pronounce upon publicly, in or outside of China—*unless* those so doing are protagonists of the ideologies and objectives advocated at a given moment by the ruling group in the Kuomintang and that party's creation, the Chungking government. Members of this powerful group would comprehend with enthusiastic approval the feelings and sentiments of that American who remarked that he would like to see an impartial history of the United States written from the southern point of view.

The paper presented by Dr. Liu constitutes a point of departure from which one can, like the hero of a certain story, ride rapidly in all directions—which is to say, that a considerable number of debatable aspects of Kuomintang China are brought into partial focus, but not photographed.

In the discussion of the paper several details and principles were added which to a greater or less degree clarified matters positively or negatively. By inference, for example, as the numbers and increasing powers of the chairmanships and other positions held by Generalissimo Chiang Kai-shek were mentioned, it became reasonably clear to students of history, if it had not hitherto so appeared, that something in the nature of a rough analogy or an approximate parallel exists between the rise to supreme authority (through the assumption of all important offices and ultimate control of all channels of influence) by Chiang in twentieth-century China and that by Augustus in first-century Rome. The generalissimo is, for example, chairman of the Supreme Council of National Defense and of the Supreme Committee of National Defense (which committee is all-powerful) and of the National Military Council and of the National Commission on Aeronautical Affairs. He is simultaneously chairman of the Central Executive Committee of the Kuomintang and of that committee's Standing Committee of seventeen members. He is also concurrently head of the Executive Yüan, which is, by all odds, the most influential of the five Yüans. Finally, consequent upon the death, in August, 1943, of Lin Sen, chairman of the National Government, the generalissimo was elected to that office which, somewhat similar to the presidency under the late third French Republic, was, until the election of the generalissimo in September, 1943, without executive functions—but not completely lacking in prestige.

In reality, however, it was not to the dignified office without power held by the late Lin Sen that the generalissimo was unanimously elected by the eighty-eight attending members of the ninth general meeting in Chungking of the eleventh plenary session of the Fifth Central Executive Committee of the Kuomintang. Contemporaneously with the election of the generalissimo, several articles of China's Organic Law of 1927 were revised to make the president of the National Government "Head of the Republic of China"; to permit him to "represent the Republic of China in foreign relations"; to make him "Commander-in-Chief of the land, naval, and air forces"; to permit him to "hold office for three years and he may be reappointed provided, however, that after the enforcement of a Permanent Constitution and upon the inauguration of the president elected he shall be relieved of his office. . . . . In case the President of the National Government is incapacitated by any cause the President of the Executive Yüan shall act on his behalf." According to Article 14 of the revised Organic Law, the president has to sign "All laws promulgated and all mandates issued by the National Government." Article 15 of the same revised law provides: "The presidents and vice-presidents of the five Yüan . . . . shall be selected and appointed by the Central Executive Committee of the Kuomintang of China from among the State Councillors recommended by the President of the National Government. The President of the National Government shall be responsible to the Central Executive Committee of the Kuomintang of China and the Presidents of the five Yüan shall be responsible to the President of the National Government." A minimum of concentration upon the facts here set forth makes clear how different is the office acceded to by the generalissimo from that held by the late Lin Sen, first president of the National Government of China.[1]

Discussion of Professor Liu's paper brought forth certain additional ideas and conclusions from the leader and from the participants at his round table, e.g., the extreme unlikelihood that, within a predictable period, the Kuomintang will be reduced to the status of a mi-

[1] Cf. *Shanghai Evening Post and Mercury* (Amer. ed., New York), I, No. 37 (September 17, 1943), 1, 4, 6.

nority party; that the general method of obtaining membership in the party is by means of introduction into the lower branches of the party organization; that there are in existence "other small groups," for example, "the Communist Party is in existence and there are some other small parties[2] . . . . the National Socialist Par-

[2] A series of articles on government and politics in wartime China by Guenther Stein, published in the *Far Eastern Survey*, Vol. XI (1942); and T. A. Bisson's "China's Part in a Coalition War" in the same periodical, Vol. XII, No. 14 (July 14, 1943); as well as *Red Star over China* (New York, 1938) and *Battle for Asia* (New York, 1941) by Edgar Snow; *Battle Hymn of China* (New York, 1943) by Agnes Smedley; and Paul M. A. Linebarger's *The China of Chiang K'ai-shek* (Boston, 1941) may well be consulted on several points discussed above. The following quotation from Mr. Stein's article "Peoples Political Council Reorganizing" (*op. cit.*, XI, No. 14 [July 13, 1942], 158–60) is especially apropos: "The Peoples Political Council, created early in 1938 'in order to unify national strength; to utilize the best minds of the nation and to facilitate the formulation and execution of national policies,' is now undergoing its third transformation. . . . . When it was first established, the P.P.C. consisted of 200 members, all of whom were appointed through the Kuomintang by organs of the National Government. Half of them were to represent the different provinces and municipalities of China, as well as Mongolia and Tibet; the other half were appointed from 'those who have served more than three years in representative cultural and economic bodies or have long devoted themselves to political activities and thereby contributed to national welfare.' Among the latter group there was a considerable number of persons not belonging to the Kuomintang, many of them representing other parties *without legal standing such as the Communist Party, the National Socialist Party, the Youth Party and the 'Third Party'* [editor's italics].

"In its reorganization in 1941, the number of members was increased to 240. Of these, 102 members for provinces, municipalities, Mongolia, Tibet, and organizations of Overseas Chinese were *elected*; 138 were still directly *appointed* by the government from the same groups as before. In every case, however, the final choice and approval of members was made by the Supreme National Defense Council, in consultation with the Central Executive Committee of the Kuomintang. . . . .

"Under the current reorganization, total membership . . . . will still be 240. The group of elected representatives from provinces and municipalities, however, is to be increased to 180, while that of appointed representatives . . . . is to be reduced to 60. . . . . The P.P.C. is supposed to meet twice a year for ten days, but traveling difficulties in China, and in the present case the reorganization, have made it impossible to adhere to that schedule. . . . ."

ty, the Youth, and so on," *but* that there are "no elec-
tions in wartime"—although it is possible for non-
Kuomintang members to be appointed to the People's
Political Council; that "there is a 'party' of non-party
members that is considered very important,—non-party, non-sectarian. Even in the People's [Political]
Council, there are certain votes allotted to that group
of non-party members . . . . that acts as a certain
check on the work of the government. But if you definitely belong to the Communist Party, then you have
not a very good chance to get into the government. If
you are a non-party member, then you are allowed to
take certain positions in the government"; that the
"People's Political Council has exerted some influence
on the work of the government. That Council meets
. . . . about once or twice a year and when that Council is in session every Minister has to make a report of
the work that he has done in the past and what he plans
to do in the future. After the report, the Council has a
resolution passed on it to point out the merits and the
defects of the work that has been done and those reso-
lutions are published in the newspapers, so, in this way,
. . . . public opinion is brought to bear on the work of
the government. And, then, after the oral report of
every Minister, members of the People's Political
Council can ask questions . . . . and sometimes they
ask very embarrassing questions. And those questions
are also published in the newspapers, so that is another
way that public opinion can be brought to bear on the
work of the government"; that "formerly the influence
of the family was very great upon the members of the
family but in recent times . . . . the influence has be-

come much smaller" and no longer appears likely to "interfere with loyalty to the State"; that one of the results of the splitting of families by migrations from Occupied to Unoccupied China has been to make many people increasingly dependent upon the government who otherwise would depend on the big family unit; that the Siamese-twin relationship at present existing between the Kuomintang and the National Government in Chungking gives to these organizations a legal right to control the national army which the Communists lack with respect to their armed forces, but that, after all, the Chinese people are interested less in the question of which party, Kuomintang or Communist, controls the country than they are in that of good government versus bad government—and that after Sino-Japanese hostilities cease there will be no struggle between the parties if the "government is good, if it is constructive and tries to improve the standard of living of the people"; but that "if the government is corrupt and seems bad in the eyes of the people, then . . . . there is very probably a chance that we shall have, perhaps, a succession of revolutions, and the question that worries non-party members is which party will be able to organize a good government? . . . . We are not in a position to speculate as to whether the Communist Party, if they come to power, will organize a better government. And, because of this, most of the Chinese intelligent class would rather hope to have a reform of the present government instead of a revolution and the taking of another chance to see what the Communists will work out in China"; that, perhaps, it is not a question of "good government versus bad government" but one of which party has the greatest power: "Most likely the Kuomintang will have the upper hand . . . . [as it] is probably much better equipped as far as fighting with other parties is concerned. . . . . The question, however, is whether Russia helps or not. . . . . If Russia helps, it is no longer a question of civil war between the Kuomintang and the Communists; it is probably a war between a part of China and another part of China and another nation as well . . . . if the Chinese Communist Party is left alone and the Kuomintang is left in its present position, most likely there won't be any civil war. . . . .

". . . . That is to say, no matter what the split-hair definition of democracy is, America is a democracy—is so in comparison with Germany, with Italy, with Japan—and there is a question . . . . as to whether China is a democracy. Well, from the point of view of institutions, China is not a democracy. But, suppose you divide the nations on the earth, and let's say whether China is nearer Japan and Germany, or whether China is somewhere near England and America: I think, on the whole, we shall say that China is much nearer to America and England than to Japan and Germany."

V

In the ageless light of history, of possibly greater consequence to China and to the rest of the world than the problems of politics are the problems of health discussed in part at the second round-table conference. Nations can survive almost any form of government, and philosophy of government, since forms and theories of state tend to change in conformity to the needs and the genius of a people. Diet and disease, however, tend to change the people themselves and, hence, their state forms and ideologies.

The specialists who reported on public health directed attention to factors of the utmost importance, for example: the generally low protein (especially animal protein) content of Chinese diet; the vitamin deficiency; the incidence of goiter (a problem in certain areas of Central Asia which interested Marco Polo in the thirteenth century); the more and the less obvious effects upon the diet of excessively low income of vast numbers of the people—and certain effects of current Sino-Japanese hostilities upon Occupied and Unoccupied China; the failure of government and people to avail themselves of existing opportunities to obtain balanced diets; the strides taken since 1928 in initiating public health measures through considerable sections of the country—but the to-be-expected continuance, nevertheless, of epidemics on a fairly wide scale; the high rate of infant mortality; the effects of transportational difficulties and inflation upon the presence and the price of drugs ("the conditions in China as to medical supplies are really very bad; the sulfa drugs which you can get here for small sums [about two United States cents a tablet] out there are up to $50 [i.e., $2.50 United States currency] a tablet; a small bottle of cod-liver oil or halibut liver oil which would be enough for a baby for a month or two would be $1,200; they are so scarce and so very expensive that nobody can touch them . . . . ; a tablet of quinine is worth several dollars . . . . ; food prices have gone up fifty to a hundred times since the war began in 1937, so that a pound of rice which used to be 10 cents now is $5.00 . . . . ; gasoline is $700 a gallon, which is $35 of your [United States] money . . . . , and a tire . . . . almost a year ago was $10,000"); the high rate of births and of infant mortality with the lack of governmental encouragement of birth control; the attempt of the Army Medical Administration "to introduce venereal prophylaxis," which has brought "so much discussion on moral grounds that it has always been turned down so that the rate of venereal disease is pretty high"; the proportion of "one doctor to 40,000 population" in China—and of one doctor to 700 population in the United States.

To the interesting question: "I'd like to ask Dr. [J. Heng] Liu if he had a choice between medical supplies and added medical personnel, which would he choose," Dr. Liu replied: ". . . . We'd prefer to have more medical supplies—because a foreign doctor in the Chinese Army is a very unhappy person. Even in Red Cross work he is a very unhappy man. It is very difficult for him to stand that sort of life. It is much worse than what you hear about Guadalcanal and Bataan; it is really bad. He wants some milk or butter or Cocacola or chewing gum or cigarets—and all that sort of thing which cannot be gotten for him. Then the question of language is, of course, a very important one: to provide him with an interpreter is an impossibility, and to get along without any language at all is a terrible handicap—so that, altogether, it is very difficult for us to make use of a foreign doctor."

When the day arrives for the composing of an unexpurgated history of will o' the wisps through the ages, that of the unlimited and innumerable fortunes to be derived by non-Chinese from trade with the Middle Country will rank as does the name of Abou Ben Adhem in the list of those who loved his fellow-men. Despite the ages-long divergent dietetic preferences of his own people and those of the Mongols, Dr. Tsai advocated wide-scale development of dairy products' consumption in China. He can have derived small consolation, however, from the remark of Dr. J. Heng Liu: "In regard to dairy products, Dr. Chu and I, who were delegates at the Hot Springs Food Conference, said that we could not see the possibility of China's using dairy products to any considerable extent for many years to come." But Dr. Liu's next remarks must be added to those which have caused hope to agitate human breasts: "We did include in the requirements of Chinese diets a certain amount of milk powder, or evaporated, or condensed, milk for infants and children, but for grown-ups we felt that it is an impossibility for many years to come. The Australians, of course, are very much interested in the export of surplus dairy products. The small amount of milk powder which we included in the requirements— something like two or three ounces a day per infant, or child, until he is five—would mean over a million tons of milk powder. That is just for children under school age. It would mean over a million tons of milk powder.

"That was figured out by the gentlemen from Australia who were so interested in the export of the milk. That shows the size of the problem in China. I mean, where we have over four hundred million people and so many per cent are children under a certain age, when we give them a couple of ounces of milk powder a day, it is very little. It is reasonable. But when you add it up and figure it out on a calculating machine, there are the figures we get. And you can imagine how much organization and capital and everything it would take to produce that much milk per year!"

A few years ago the cloth manufacturers of Manchester were calculating, probably without the use of new-fangled calculating machines, how many more millions of yards of cloth would be sold in China "if every Chinaman would only lengthen his gown two inches." Thus are will o'the wisps born; and will o'the wisps, like other ideals, are lovely and graceful and of good report—but it is pleasanter to think upon their births and development than upon their deaths. However, as in the case of human deaths, it is comforting to remember that births go on forever.

VI

Of the voices from Unoccupied China, whose dicta make up this volume, none spoke with more authority and clarity of objective than that of Dr. Wu in his discussion of "Economic Reconstruction and Planning: Wartime and Post-war." Nowhere else, it may be added, has the determination of Chungking to industrialize China—be the cost what it may in human lives, human misery, human energy, and vastness of financial expenditures—been more definitely, and apparently irrevocably, set forth. If the earlier cited articles by T. A. Bisson and Guenther Stein and the studies of contemporary China by Paul M. A. Linebarger, Edgar Snow, and Agnes Smedley admirably supplement Dr. N. C. Liu's exposition of the Chungking government, no less important for supplementary reading to Dr. Wu's outline of plans for China's industrialization is Ralph Borsodi's "Must China Endure This Too?" (with its subheading, "The Evils of Industrialism Can and Must Be Avoided by the Chinese People Who Have the Chance To Modernize without Falling Victims to the 'Great Illusion' Which Has Plunged the Western Nations and Japan into Insecurity, Imperialism, and War") in *Asia and the Americas*, XLIII, No. 9 (September, 1943), 539–44.

What Dr. Wu looks upon as advantageous for his country, Mr. Borsodi views with horrified apprehension for its effect upon the people. Because of the smallness of the farms ("the average size of farms in China as a whole is 22 mow, which equals only $3\frac{1}{2}$ acres"), Dr. Wu advocates migration of unnumbered millions to the cities and enlargement of farms for those who remain in the countryside. But, argues Mr. Borsodi, "those who are recommending the industrialization of China, as a means of improving the conditions of life for the Chinese people, should face the corollaries of their recommendation. For the revolution to which they have committed themselves involves the substitution of an industrial for an agrarian civilization, the destruction of organic village life in order to make possible the development of modern manufacturing centers, and the abolition of a culture based upon the family in order to enable a culture to develop in which the individual becomes a unit of an atomized and anonymous metropolitan society. More immediately, the protagonists of industrialism must frankly admit that they would commit China to: (1) a huge capital investment in the billions . . . . ;

(2) secondly, huge profits—or margins above operating expenses must be permitted in these enterprises . . . . ; (3) the capital investment . . . . must be devoted to the development of transportation and distribution as against manufacturing in the ratio of not less than five to one . . . . and ultimately not less than ten to one . . . . ; (4) the whole economy, and ultimately the entire culture, of China must be transformed in order to enable its proposed factory system to survive . . . . ; (5) finally, the present regional and local organization of Chinese economy, politics, and culture must be replaced by a standardized nationalized society. . . . .

"The fact is that industrialism is so costly, exploitive, destructive, and inefficient that no nation has ever adopted it except by making an investment of incalculable human misery. . . . .

"The protagonists of Chinese industrialism would have poor China jump out of the frying pan of medievalism into the fire of industrialism. Their fundamental error is their assumption that the theory of the division of labor gives them no other alternative if China is to progress and the Chinese standard of living to be raised. The fact of the matter, however, is that there is another alternative. *China may be modernized without being industrialized.*"

The potentially crucial role of the Chinese industrial co-operatives in the bringing-about of the alternative suggested is briefly discussed. Perhaps by accident, perhaps for reasons which were not manifested, the history, contemporary status, and possible future development

of the industrial co-operatives were scarcely touched upon by the Harris Foundation conference leaders.[3]

The combined suggestion and query was offered:
"Isn't the labor supply in the cities already adequate?
If you look at the solution that is generally proposed,
that the problems of agriculture can be solved by pro-
viding urban jobs, factory jobs for the farm population,
you find the rest of the world has never been able to do
it. . . . . If you move your population from the country to the city, then you have an economic depression—
and the next thing you do is to move your idle laborers
back to subsistence farms. Where do you get with the
general proposition that you move the country people
in to the places where the labor supply is already adequate?"

To this Dr. Wu replied, "I should think that our condition is a little different from what prevails in other
countries. We are an agricultural country and the majority of our population lives on the farms—I think
from 75 to 80 per cent. This kind of distribution I
don't think is very healthy. Of course we don't want to
put 80 per cent of our population in the cities, either,
but I think we can get, say, 20 to 30 per cent more of
our population in the cities or in the small-sized towns,
instead of crowding them all in the rural districts. . . . .
We hope to achieve that goal by reducing our proportion of farmers from 75 per cent to 50 per cent in about
thirty years."

[3] This statement applies also to the immeasurable influence of Western
Christian missionaries, particularly American and English, upon modern education in China and the modernizing of the country in the nineteenth and
twentieth centuries.

On this problem, Dr. Fei remarked that he might be able to "add some observations . . . . from the factories around Kunming [Yünnan]. We had a study of this problem . . . . and they tried to find out how far the farmers can directly join in factory work. . . . . It was very inefficient for the farmer to get a job in the factory. In the last three years, the management of the modern factories in that part of China decided to stop putting farmers in the factories and to try to train their partly skilled labor direct from the youngsters of twelve years old or so. In this way they can really have a basis for skilled labor rather than taking the rural labor into the factory. The part-time worker in the factory is really a problem for the management. It has proved costly to the management."

To Dr. Fei's observation Dr. Wu did not reply; but, commenting upon the estimated 180,000,000–280,000,-000 acres of cultivated land in all China, including Manchuria, he remarked: "That amount of cultivated land is about the same size as the cultivated land in this country. Maybe your cultivated land is even a little greater than ours, but in this country you use only 10,000,000 farmers to do the job, while we use . . . . about 140,000,000 . . . . and I think one way to increase the efficiency is to enlarge their farms and to put them to some other line of work such as transportation, or factory work, or mines, or public works. That is why I want to take out a certain percentage of the rural population and put them in other occupations—thereby increasing the standard of living of the farmers." A bit later Dr. Wu added: "From the point of view of raising the standard of living we should pay more attention to the yield per person rather than the yield per acre . . . . there is a lot to be done in improving the farming methods[4] . . . . but with that small farm, no matter what you do, there is really little hope of raising their standard to such a point that they can send their children to the middle schools, for example. That is why in Chinese society their vertical mobility is really very, very slow and it takes . . . . generations to raise the status of the family. If you want to be in a school, you have to start with your grandfather. Maybe he may send his son to a shop to be an apprentice, thereby getting some more money, and he may learn some reading and arithmetic in the store. Then he will realize the importance of education, and he will send *his* son to the school, and maybe, when it comes to the third generation, he can improve his status a little bit. That is because of this difficulty of accumulating any capital with this small farm. You can hardly change your status in your lifetime, and I think that is one of our main troubles with our farmers. . . . . I don't want to leave the impression that from now on we are going to neglect the farms altogether. I think these two processes should go hand in hand—that is, improving the farming methods and at the same time trying to get industrialization as quickly as possible . . . ." —by government action and by private enterprise.

Writing on the subject of population pressure in China during the early years of the republic, Mr. J. O. P. Bland pointed out the relation between this phenomenon and what he termed the "procreative reck-

---

[4] On this subject consult Professor J. Lossing Buck's *Land Utilization in China* (Shanghai, 1937).

lessness" of the Chinese people. With reference to this problem, Dr. Wu observed: "It is very difficult to advocate birth control just at the present. The new Ministry of Social Affairs has formed a committee on social policy, and they invited all the professors of sociology . . . . to serve as members. . . . . I think all of us [sociologists] advocate birth control, but the rest [i.e., "some members of the legislature and some other officials"] are against it. So we had a debate for two or three sessions—and, finally, we came to this conclusion: that we are not going to use the words 'birth control,' but will use the words 'spacing of the family.' . . . . I think we got this idea over and they will allow this practice. If a person knows the methods of birth control, he is not going to have a very large family. So, as a result, I think we can achieve the same purpose."

Apropos of this subject, an American participant in Dr. Fei's round table later suggested that "with the improvement of sanitation, and without the adequate spacing that you referred to today, it would seem to me that your population on the farm would grow about as rapidly as you could remove it from the farm to the factory." To this Dr. Fei replied: "I think so. My landlord had seven children; only three of them are living now; but, with better income and better sanitation, if I am still living in this house for ten years, then I think there will be at least seven again." Dr. Wu added: "I think the public health work that Dr. Chu and Dr. Liu are doing will also cut down the death rate so that the final result will be a natural increase in population. On the other side, ... the extension of education will bring down the birth rate; that will bring about later marriage. So . . . . that in the next twenty or thirty years we may expect some increase in population—but after that the rate of increase will be much slower. . . . . I think I may [also] mention another factor which may retard the growth of our population. That is, the unequal sex distribution of our population. According to our statistics, we have at present about forty million more males than females. That is one of the reasons why Dr. Fei mentioned [that] there are so many old bachelors in our villages. But you seldom meet any old maids. And you find many monks and very few nuns. Many Chinese cannot get married because of this unequal distribution. . . . ."

To the query concerning what has happened to "the modern code of laws which has forbidden simultaneous plurality of marriages" in China, in contrast to the "consecutive polygamy such as we have in the United States," Dr. Fei succinctly replied: "It lies sleeping now!" A reply which is thought-stimulating for various reasons, not least so in the light of the previously reported existence in China of "about forty million more males than females." Likewise worthy of meditation upon in the night watches is the statement that "nearly every one of them [i.e., "high officials"] is against birth control," partly because "in the books written by Dr. Sun Yat-sen he had a few pages pointing out that the natural increase of China is much lower than those of other countries, so there is a danger [!] in China of decreasing population" and partly because "many people also confuse this issue with the moral issue (they will say that if you teach this method to the younger generation they will go wild and sow wild oats everywhere, and that is not very moral)," and partly because "the war situation at the present will affect the idea because we have lost so many men and we have to make up for that loss," and also because "there are still many government officials who believe that China's war strength depends upon the numbers of population rather than upon the industrialization of the nation."

Out of queries regarding "limiting profits of private enterprise" and the extraordinarily high interest rates prevailing in China, the belief was expressed that "nearly all the factories in Chungking make more than 20 per cent" and that after the war "attempts will probably be made to impose limits on private enterprise" but that "during the time of inflation if you limit the profit rate to say 20 per cent, then no factories will open their doors. They will just hold up the raw materials and wait for a few months, when they will get more than 20 per cent profit. . . . . Because of inflation, you can always make a very high profit by holding the materials . . . . [also] if you should lower the interest rates, then the banks will lose money because they pay interest to those who make deposits—in Szechuan Province, for example, sometimes at 15 per cent . . . ." —or even 30 per cent, according to another commentator.

Dr. Wu's suggestion that the United States shall lend to China, at the close of the war, "some of the $15,000,000,000 worth of wartime industrial plants" which it has built and owns, was followed by questions concerning, for example, management of the factories (if it were possible to transport them to China) by government or by private enterprise and compensation for such factories. To which the proposer of the suggestion replied, in part: ". . . . The government wants to play a more important rôle in the field of heavy industries, leaving the consumer industries in the hands of the private enterprisers. . . . . All these plants owned by the [United States] government have been paid for already, so you don't need to impose any more burden on the taxpayers if you should lend some of the plants to China. For the present year, aircraft factories are producing more than seven thousand airplanes per month. I don't think you will need that many airplanes after the war. Instead of scrapping the machinery, I think it is much better to lend it to China. . . . . Of course, we are going to repay the debt. We are not going to ask charity. That is quite evident. But we want a long-term loan—say, twenty or thirty years. And I think we can get that more easily from the government than from private banks. . . . . We want to talk business with this country, but we want to talk business in a very friendly spirit and not in the spirit of *The Merchant of Venice!* That is, we want to get a long-term loan and at very low interest, so that our finance will not be burdened by debt, particularly during the first few years. But in the future, with your help, I think we can increase our production, and maybe twenty or thirty years later we can have more exports than imports, and thereby repay our debt. . . . ."

VII

The probable failure of an attempt to solve the problem of population pressure in China by drawing off excessive numbers of rural inhabitants to work in great urban factories (not, of course, that population pressure

constitutes the *basic* reason for China's proposed industrialization), which was implied by Dr. Fei in his
remark concerning training twelve-year-olds rather
than rural adults for factory life, was even more clearly
implicit in the reference, in his round-table paper,
"Some Social Problems of Free China," to the "traditional ideology of filial prosperity—of having many
sons—which must [in the frontier provinces] have been
as sufficiently effective as elsewhere in China to bring
up the size of the population in a short period to its saturation point. . . . . At present the frontier provinces
constitute no exception to the generalization made by
Professor Tawney that 'the population of China is too
large to be supported by existing resources.'" It seems
fairly clear that (aside from encouraging) migration,
urbanization, and industrialization have, thus far, not
notably affected Chinese will to procreation. Widespread wars, floods, droughts, and famines have had
considerable effects upon its results.[5]

One of the most significant changes touched on by
Dr. Fei was that of the contemporaneously lowered
economic (and, quite possibly, social and political)
status of the scholar in China. The full meaning of this
can be comprehended only by those informed concerning scholarly status during the ages. "I think our conception of classes is a little different from that of other
countries," Dr. Wu remarked during a discussion of
present-day changes in Chinese economic and social institutions—changes exemplified by a situation in which
day laborers in parts of Unoccupied China now receive

[5] Cf., e.g., W. H. Mallory, *China: Land of Famine* (New York, 1926), and
H. F. MacNair, *With the White Cross in China* (Peking, 1939).

a higher income than college professors. "Our ancient sage who put the scholar above other classes was not using a pecuniary standard for measurement. Scholars like Confucius were not rich persons, but they had vision, culture, wisdom—and you achieve that status through pursuit of knowledge and not through pursuit of money. Therefore, even when the scholars are poor, they still feel they have a very dignified position in the social organization.[6] . . . . Last year, in both Kunming and Chungking, there was a movement to revive the old idea concerning scholars. Many articles have been written . . . . pointing out the function of a scholar in society and trying to boost up the spirit—or the morale—of the scholars . . . . and there are many professors and engineers in the government directing industries. . . . . I should say that those who have undergone training in the universities both in China and abroad are looked upon as scholars in the old sense, even the engineers."

To a question regarding the value of the scholar in the marriage market, Dr. Fei replied: "I think I had better answer this by a concrete case that occurred in our vil-

---

[6] Later in the discussion Dr. Chin called attention to the fact that "Confucius did not initiate [respect for] the scholars. There were scholars before Confucius' time. Confucius was one of the scholars; he belonged to the scholar class. Earlier the scholar was one of a class of people that could do certain things—who could write certain things, who could perform ceremonies, who could perform religious ceremonies and funeral ceremonies and, probably, marriage ceremonies. . . . . The scholar is a class of people, not necessarily noted for scholarship but a class of people which satisfies certain functions and those functions have something to do with writing and reading.

"For instance, if you are worshiping God, worshiping your ancestors, probably you find some kind of writing there. You may be performing a funeral service. A scholar [in days of old] was one who knew the rites, who knew the customs, who read the old manuscripts and that sort of thing."

lage, in our Research Institute. I have a group of bachelors staying with me in the country. We set up a little Research Institute there. Once an old lady of the peasants came to make a match for one of my Research Fellows with a girl in her village, and she said to him, 'You will have so many mow of land and you will secure a good life.' And I encouraged my student to consider it. That struck me as interesting. That would not have been possible in the past. It was ridiculous, but such a proposal was actually made."

"QUESTION: What was not possible in the past?

"ANSWER: For a peasant to marry a college graduate!

"QUESTION: Yes, but the peasant was rich!

"ANSWER: Even if she is rich! I don't know why, but I think that is rather ridiculous. I was quite surprised at the occurrence.

"QUESTION: Then your argument, if I follow it correctly, is that the intellectual is low in the marriage market?

"ANSWER: That is why there are bachelors everywhere. They just remain unmarried. They cannot get any sort of girl—even the professors in the university."

Dr. Y. L. Chin remarked: "With regard to your question, I think there is still a sort of admiration for scholarship, or the scholar class. One of the young men of the Academia Sinica got married to the daughter of the landlady. He was extremely poor.

"QUESTION: Because of the local situation, or because he had always been poor?

"DR. CHIN: I don't know whether he had always been poor or not, but he has been poor for the last few years. In fact, he didn't have the money to get married. The lady's family got them married.

"After a few months or so the lady became quite dissatisfied and one day, during the Anniversary of the Academia Sinica . . . . the Director of that particular institute had a bright idea. He gave a speech there. He said, 'The Academia Sinica has a position corresponding to the Hanlin Yüan in the old Ts'ing dynasty'—Hanlin being the highest scholarly rank. So he compared the Academia Sinica with the Hanlin Yüan and he said, 'All these Research Fellows are actually Hanlins in the Republic.'

"After that speech, it seemed that the family differences of the newlyweds disappeared miraculously. So that there still is a good deal of that kind of admiration for the scholarly positions."

Dr. Fei added: "The case I cited, I think, indicates the possibility of the rich landlord coming up and marrying his daughter to somebody whom he admired. That is why he comes in to talk match-making.

"QUESTION: Take another entirely different case. Let's take the rich manufacturer, or a man who has made his fortune from the war. Will he wish to marry his daughter to either a returned student or a college graduate of a Chinese institution?

"DR. FEI: That I don't know.

"DR. N. C. LIU: I think they will gladly do that.

"DR. WU: I think they will be very glad to do it."

The tendency on the part of some to view scholarship from the utilitarian, rather than the cultural-humanitarian, point of view or, to state it slightly differently,

to attempt to mold the scholar into a tool or technician
of the state rather than to continue looking upon him as
a policy-forming, impartial philosopher-adviser in the
functioning of government, central and local, is apparent. Such a trend is obviously away from the ages-old
Chinese conception of the position and duties of scholars in the ages-old scholastic state, and seems to constitute a move toward transforming scholars into props
for a type of state as different from that of ancient times
as a state based on modern industry is from a state built
on an ancient culture.

On the philological (not ethical) basis that morality
is that which is consonant with established custom while
immorality is that which is not consonant with established custom, Dr. Fei commented, directly and indi-
rectly, upon the growth of "immorality" in Unoccupied
China. This has resulted in the main from the latest
Sino-Japanese war with consequent moving into the
western provinces of vast numbers of people from the
more modernized parts of the country. The youth, for
example, who ran away from home three times to avoid a
family-arranged marriage in accord with custom is im-
moral from the viewpoint of his parents and their
friends but is admired by his younger brothers and his
friends. "The old morals are breaking down and a new
set of moral codes is in formation," remarked Dr. Wu.
"One of our former colleagues, Dr. Fung [Yu-lan], at
present head of the department of philosophy in Tsinghua University, is writing a book called "The New Morals," trying to form a new moral code and preaching this
kind of moral code for the adoption of the younger
generation. . . . . Trying to fit it into the new situa-

tion, to industrialize society, calling on the general population to pay more attention to the affairs of the country and to be more patriotic, and other things which are neglected by the old teachings. . . . . In Dr. Fung's new book I think he pays more attention to patriotism than to filial piety."

Commenting upon the difference between the present-day situation with respect to morals in Unoccupied China and that which prevailed in the Wu-han area, in the Yangtze Valley, and other parts of the country in 1927, and for a time thereafter, Dr. Fei was of the opinion that "there was a conscious attack on the existing morals during that [1927] period of revolution. Now it is different. There is not an organized movement against morals. On the contrary, government and most of the elders are trying to maintain the old codes. This has developed strongly during the war. . . . . I think an attack on the traditional moral code to fit it to sanction the new way of life is better than to hang one's self on the old standards—and see the boys and girls run wild. It is better to follow [and direct] the current than to stand and criticize it."

The discussion, at Dr. Fei's round table, of the universal and ages-old conflict now being waged in China between "old" and "new" customs and consequent moral systems and over rural problems, population pressure, and plans for industrialization ended with the following questions, posed by American participants, and Dr. Wu's replies:

"QUESTION: If you are planning industrialization, and if you contemplate that that may mean increased population, where is the food coming from?

"ANSWER: That depends upon the standard. If we follow the more advanced Western standard, then, of course, there will not be enough food, but if we still cling to the old standard, I think there are many ways to increase our food supply. For example, the dissemination of better seeds. I am told that by that process alone we can increase our food supply 20 per cent. And in the past I think, although we imported some wheat or rice, that the amount has never been more than 5 per cent of the home production.

"QUESTION: You figure on exportation of industrial products in exchange for food?

"ANSWER: By using better seeds we can grow more rice and more wheat on a certain area, and by eradication of pests I am told they can increase another 50 per cent, and by irrigation can still further increase the food supply.

"QUESTION: You contemplate mechanization of agriculture also, so that the same number of people can raise more food—can use more land?

"ANSWER: That will come much later because our farms are too small to use any mechanized implements.

"QUESTION: Even after they have been increased in size, as you expect?

"ANSWER: We have to increase our farms five or six times. Then we may talk about mechanization. But at present Dr. Fei pointed out that we have surpluses of labor in farming. Even with the enlargement of farms, we can still use the laborers in the country without using any mechanized help at all.

"QUESTION: Does that mean that the standard of living, if the population increases and you can produce only that much more food, would increase so that Chinese will be able to buy American products?

"ANSWER: I think we realize very well that this population problem is one of our big problems in China, and we cannot see very clearly just how we are going to solve it, since there is such a psychological resistance against the dissemination of the knowledge of birth control.

"I hope that maybe twenty or thirty years later, with the greater industrialization and the greater education that will come, it will come naturally, after all."

VIII

The relation of education to the divers topics and problems touched upon at the four round tables referred to above led logically to a general survey of that topic at the concluding section of the institute. As logically Dr. Yueh-lin Chin led the discussion, speaking informally, as had Dr. J. Heng Liu.

No more surprising fact eventuated than the first one to be mentioned, namely, that, during the years of war with Japan since 1937, the number of students in China has notably increased. Not surprising is the second point discussed, namely, that, while "quantity" has increased, quality has equally notably declined. Under the conditions prevailing—with removal from school and university buildings, and their destruction or taking-over for other purposes than education by the invaders, and with loss of books, scientific apparatus, and other educational equipment, and with students and faculties trekking hundreds of miles into the interior to establish themselves in new and adequate surroundings—

maintenance of pre-war standards was impossible. For a long generation, since the outbreak of the anti-Manchu, pro-Republic revolution of 1911-12, education has suffered. Twice within this generation—in the years 1925-27, and in 1931-37 (with the occurrence of the so-called Mukden Incident) to the present—carefully planned and not indifferently executed assaults upon education have taken place throughout vast areas of the republic. Instead, however, of destroying, or even dangerously crippling, education, these assaults have demonstrated that persecution, bloodshed, and martyrdom stimulate heroism and growth in realms of the spirit other than the purely religious. Like religion, on occasion, education has suffered—and prospered.

The element of whimsical humor which permeated the gravity of Dr. Chin's analyses was illustrated by his remarks in concluding the first part of his discussion: 'Last night Mr. Teng was very, very anxious as to whether there would be any questions, and he said, 'If there are no questions what are we going to do?' We have a conflicting interest, you see. I did not say it to him, but I said it to myself: 'Suppose there *are* questions, what am *I* going to do?' "

An interesting apparent illustration, at least in part, of the innumerable transferences to Asia of Western national rivalries since the sixteenth century was given in connection with the difficulties faced by certain professors of engineering who, on escaping in 1937 from Peking (or P'eiping—whichever one wishes: the name changes with the tides of politics and war) went to Nanking to offer their services to the War Department—and "couldn't get into the War Department." With respect to which apparent anomaly, Dr. Wu volunteered: "I think of one explanation in this case. That is the Office of Ordnance. It happens that the head of that department is a German-returned student, and, I think, all of their engineers are German-returned students. The man of whom Dr. Chin speaks is American-returned, and they may think that in that office they should use only German-returned students because of the German terms, and they talk German most of the time. . . . . It is easier for them to get along with engineers trained in Germany."

Following reminiscence of a somewhat similar experience undergone by another scientist who attempted to offer his services, the remark was made: "I take it from what you say that the government is not using the universities as we are doing in this country—to train personnel for specific jobs in the war? That is, you aren't using universities to do the kind of thing that we are doing here at the University of Chicago, for example?

"ANSWER: No. Certainly not in Kunming. I don't know whether it is true in other universities, but it is not true in Kunming. Excepting for one thing. Because of the presence of the 14th Army Air Corps, a large number of translators are needed and the Western Language Department of the university is supplying a large number of translators.

"ANOTHER PARTICIPANT: I would say that the medical-school students were conscripted for two years' service. That is different from other college graduates. They [medical students] have to join the Army, the Red Cross, the public administration, for at least two years after their graduation. If you graduate and do not comply with this request of the government, a diploma will not be granted.

"ANOTHER PARTICIPANT: And in our medical school we have a new system which they call State Medicine. . . . . In our school we admit only state-service students, that is, their expenses are borne by the government entirely: their food, their uniform, etc. And they are supposed, or required, to render service to the state for twelve years after their graduation. There are now four governmental medical colleges practicing this system. It is hoped that in the near future pretty nearly all the medical colleges will follow this system.

"QUESTION: May I ask, wasn't there a precedent for that in the Normal Schools? Was it not the practice of some Normal Schools, whether they be provincial or more local, to require that graduates go into government service to teach in government schools for a certain length of time?

"ANSWER: Yes. That is still so.

"ANOTHER PARTICIPANT: The Normal School takes only state-service students. They are required to teach at least five years after their graduation. . . . .

"QUESTION: Shall we come back to education in wartime, and a special kind of education? That explains why the universities are not taking on special training courses for military purposes. I have visited several of the army training schools. The army started its own training courses, and there is a large number of students. They feel that is more efficient than trying to put this burden on the already heavily burdened professors. Also, it suits better the idea of the best leaders in the Department of War.

"In these schools they have a rather elaborate curriculum. They have divisions on an expeditionary force to Burma. They have special investigative training on how to be a spy and all these things. I think that is a part of education we must not overlook—if we call that education. That is a part which is especially adapted to the war situation.

"On the other hand, I think that certain schools are organized around returned students from Germany, others around returned students from France. It occurs to me that that is the reason why there is a tendency for students returned from America and England not to seem so welcome in the government, and on certain factory jobs, and at these other universities.

"Dr. Tsai: I do not believe that is true. . . . . I think if one is a French-returned student, he is most likely to follow the trend. It is more natural that he go with others with that same training. I think there is no discrimination in the Ministry of War to take French- or German-returned students."

The honest divergencies of opinion which are brought forth, without consequent fatalities, at Harris Foundation conferences are among the most worth-while aspects of these meetings. Two such divergencies occurred in connection with Dr. Chin's discussion. One had to do with that round-table leader's expression of mild disesteem[7] for the ancient, classical, Chinese educational system and the brief survey and balanced defense of the system for its period presented by the chairman, Dr. S. Y. Teng, assistant professor of Chinese in the Uni-

[7] Apropos of this, the following colloquy took place:
"Question: I'd like to ask Dr. Chin whether he feels any result from

versity of Chicago, and himself, like Dr. Chin, a distinguished product of the ancient Chinese and the modern Western systems of education.

The other heartening divergence was Dr. Chin's calm and impartial expression of doubt concerning certain institutional trends in contemporary China, educational and economic. He approved of neither the narrowing tendency in education manifested in the flocking of vast numbers of students "into intensely practical studies," such as engineering, at the expense of the humanities and "the old, gentle, liberal education," nor of the too speedy and too vast industrialization and mechanization of the country. "We used to have," he re-

---

that memory education. Do you feel yourself better educated from having had that than people who haven't had it?

"DR. CHIN: I, personally, do not.

"QUESTION: Do you notice that people who have had that education are any different from those who have not?

"DR. CHIN: Yes. I think I am exhibiting the effect of that now, possibly. There is one thing that seems to me to be quite distinct. Among the people who are somewhere between forty and fifty—even those who were educated in America, my schoolmates in America for instance—most of them are not skilful with their hands, for one thing, and the people who come later are much more ready with their hands. I am extremely stupid with my hands. I can't do a single thing with them. Last night I broke my watch while winding it. That is why I came here so early and stayed here: I broke my watch!

"Of course, that may be a special endowment not common to people of my age and training, ... For instance, most of the people of my age can't learn to drive an automobile, but among my friends who are between twenty-five and thirty-five, it is much easier for them to learn to drive an automobile. There is quite a lot of difference. I mean your education up the present has been along modern lines and has made that improvement.

"QUESTION: You think they haven't lost anything in not having that memory education? You don't find that their memory is better . . . . from having had that training?

"DR. CHIN: Very peculiarly, as far as the present time is concerned, in spite of my poor memory I can still recite some of the old classic things—but I have a very poor memory. And I don't know their meaning. I can still recite a bit of the *Book of Odes*, but I don't understand a single word of it—even now!"

marked, "a very strong department of physics at Tsing-hua University; it generally got the best students admitted to the university. At the present time it is difficult to attract students to the study of physics. I think this is to some extent also true of chemistry and of other pure sciences." And elsewhere he added: "No, I am not referring to research. I am referring to a definite attempt on the part of some people to discourage students from entering into the study of pure science."

On this detail Dr. Tsai, the scientist, was inclined to take issue with Dr. Chin, the humanist, following queries from American participants in the discussion as to how it could be supposed that engineers (as contrasted with technicians) could be produced without training in physics, chemistry, mathematics, and the biological sciences. Dr. Tsai declared:

"I don't think in teaching engineering they are neglecting chemistry and physics at all. Suppose a man is going to take industrial chemistry; he has to study all the subjects. I think that what Dr. Chin has in mind is that there is a lack of a group of men who wish to specialize in pure physics. But, for instance, in medicine our students are required to study biology, chemistry, etc., before they get through. They have that before anatomy, physiology, etc. There is no lack of college students of that sort. I think what Dr. Chin has in mind is those who go into pure physics. . . . . I think there is a very good number of young men going in for chemistry. The training called for by society, or by the nation, determines the question. A man can easily get a job in engineering after graduation. That is why more students study engineering than those who study pure science. The latter is taught mostly in the universities and the graduates have to become teachers in universities.

"QUESTION: Do I understand, then, that there is going to be available a good deal of training even in advanced physics or chemistry or, for that matter, on a similar level in the biological sciences, but that the trend is, in the student population, away from these subjects? . . . . You were talking of what is happening in aeronautical engineering from the point of view of the potential production of planes by yourselves. If you are going to do that, you will need not merely a great deal of physics and other related subjects but you are going to have to maintain a research establishment on the very highest level in the basic sciences that contribute to aeronautical engineering or you will not have aeronautical engineering retain a level of performance that will keep you in line with the developments elsewhere. Is that contemplated? Is that understood?

"PROFESSOR CHIN: I'm afraid it is not very thoroughly understood. That is to say, I think the importance of the allied subjects is probably not sufficiently emphasized. Consequently, I feel that, even if we establish a research bureau for aeronautical engineering, we shan't succeed because there is not sufficient background and training, not sufficient attention paid to the allied subjects.

"You see, all these things are new to China—physics, chemistry—all those things. We haven't a tradition of physics and chemistry and the pure sciences.[8] We have

[8] On this subject cf. Yu-Lan Fung, "Why China Has No Science: An Interpretation of the History and Consequences of China's Philosophy," *International Journal of Ethics*, XXXII (April, 1922), 237–63.

to develop and encourage those in order to be able to bring those things up to a certain standard, and at the present time it seems the danger is that before we attain to any kind of standard along those lines, we shall be so discouraged—these things will be so discouraged—that very few people will go in for them. I think if we overemphasize engineering as engineering and underemphasize physics and chemistry and the pure sciences, we shall not succeed.

"QUESTION: That is what I am trying to indicate, and I am wondering why, in the face of that conviction on your part—and it must be the conviction of lots of others—

"PROFESSOR CHIN (*interrupting*): I think that is not quite so. That is what I'm afraid of.

"DR. TSAI: I think this is really related. Development of industry always follows development of the pure sciences because in industry we have problems which can be solved only by physical means. At the same time, I think there is a tendency in the initial period of industrialization to copy what has been done in other, foreign, countries. So I think that the importance of physics and chemistry will naturally follow. The same situation will occur in medical schools. I am not at all pessimistic. . . . . A group of pure physicists will never get into engineering. You have to start engineering, and then create the physics later. The products of the factory will have to support the research in physics and chemistry.

"QUESTION: That is what bothers me—that you are going to start engineering without, apparently, due attention to the tools that the engineer operates with.

"DR. TSAI: I don't think we shall neglect physics at all."

Recognizing the need for a degree of "quick mechanization and industrialization for national defense," Dr. Chin added: "But what I do not like to see is the haste in which we are trying to do it. . . . . I can see consequences which would make me extremely uncomfortable, to say the least, and which, I think, will probably have a rather bad effect not alone in China but elsewhere. . . . . I myself think that we shall not succeed in industrializing ourselves sufficiently to give us the kind of security that we intend to have through the speeding-up of industrialization. . . . . The policy of encouraging engineering and economics at the expense of other subjects would not be adequate to give us a quick industrialization and mechanization so as to give us, in turn, the kind of security that we need. I, personally, am inclined to think that as far as education is concerned we have to attempt it more slowly. . . . . If we return to some of the intrinsic purposes of education . . . . the preservation of knowledge and the encouragement of knowledge, and the building-up of human character . . . . we can easily see that too much . . . . diversion of young men into one or two even admittedly useful lines will not give us the kind of citizens that some of us want."

Voicing deep and heartfelt fear of the development in his country of regimentation and totalitarianism— "which I think Americans should be afraid of, too"— Dr. Chin ended his discussion with a poignant appeal for a "world plan . . . . so that security may be given to individual nations from the point of view of the world

SYNTHESIS OUT OF ANALYSIS

as a whole; not from the point of view of an individual nation trying to attain its own security."

Those who persevere to the end of this Introduction and who then digest the messages of the seven Voices from Unoccupied China (or who read first the messages and then resort to the Introduction) will experience most of the sensations (except those connected with the heat of Chicago in midsummer) which they would have experienced had they attended the conference itself. They will, too, understand why the term "diplomatic documents" is applied by the editor to the papers herein commented upon. The quotations selected from the round-table reports throw very considerable light upon the topics formally discussed—without, it is hoped, in any wise breaking the seal of privacy, secrecy, and confidence under which Harris Foundation round-table discussions are carried on. A critical reading of the papers and the selections mentioned cannot fail to result in the obtaining by the reader of a highly significant series of facts with respect to certain contemporary conditions, events, and institutions of, possibly in the long run, the United States' most important ally among the United Nations.

HARLEY FARNSWORTH MACNAIR, *Editor*

CHICAGO
November, 1943

TABLE OF CONTENTS

INTRODUCTION: SYNTHESIS OUT OF ANALYSIS iii

THE FRAMEWORK OF GOVERNMENT IN UNOCCUPIED CHINA . 1
Liu Nai-chen, Professor of Political Science, National Wu-Han University

PROBLEMS OF NUTRITION IN PRESENT-DAY CHINA . . . 16
Tsai Chiao, Professor of Physiology, National Central University

THE MODERN PUBLIC HEALTH MOVEMENT IN CHINA . . . 26
C. K. Chu, Director of the National Institute of Health

THE ORIGIN AND DEVELOPMENT OF PUBLIC HEALTH SERVICE
IN CHINA 36
J. Heng Liu, Head of the Department of Medical Supplies, China Defense Supplies, Inc.

SOME SOCIAL PROBLEMS OF FREE CHINA 46
Fei Hsiao-t'ung, Professor of Sociology, National Yünnan University

ECONOMIC RECONSTRUCTION AND PLANNING: WARTIME AND
POST-WAR 65
Wu Ching-chao, Senior Secretary, Chinese Ministry of Economic Affairs

EDUCATION IN CONTEMPORARY CHINA 81
Chin Yueh-lin, Professor of Logic, National Tsinghua University

INDEX 101

THE FRAMEWORK OF GOVERNMENT IN UNOCCUPIED CHINA

By LIU NAI-CHEN

CONSIDERATION of what China is today politically is a task not lacking in difficulties, inasmuch as exigencies of war exert great effect upon the functions of government and upon the political life of the people.

To understand the machinery of administration of pre-war China, reference must be made to three forms of government. First, there was that of the monarchy; then that of the republic; and now there is the Five Power Constitution.

All of you know that China was a monarchy for some thousands of years. Theoretically, the emperor was extremely powerful. With the help of a few ministers about him and a small number of subordinate officials directly responsible to him, whom he sent to the provinces as governors, he ruled over his people as a father over his children. Though the ruler could in theory do anything he liked, the policy generally followed was positively to promote the well-being of the people and negatively not to disturb them. As for the people, they should be able to live peacefully and carry on their professions prosperously. Despotism was rarely carried to excess. If it was, popular opposition in the form of revolt might cause the loss of his position by the emperor and, rather probably, that of his dynasty.

With the revolution of 1911 there vanished the old form of government. China was proclaimed a republic, but the adoption of a workable political system caused great difficulties. For example, Yuan Shih-k'ai was inaugurated as first president, and the legislative assembly was dominated by the majority of the Kuomintang. Adoption of the presidential system of government would have enhanced the power of a one-man rule, while the introduction of the parliamentary system of government would have left the president a mere figurehead. Struggles for the adoption of the one rather than the other raged for several years until at last the legislature was abolished and the cabinet became nothing more than a presidential secretariat.

The cause of the failure of this political experiment was largely due to two conditions: first, lack of political consciousness on the part of the people and, second, lack of political experience on the part of the leaders.

In view of the political reaction, Dr. Sun Yat-sen came out of more or less voluntary retirement and organized several revolutionary governments in the south in opposition to that of Peking. After careful study and extensive research, Dr. Sun developed the theory of the Five Power Constitution, which suggests the conventional separation of powers and in which are embodied the principles of democratic government.

The idea was subsequently translated into a workable scheme, which is now in operation. Concretely, under this scheme supreme power was at first in the hands of the Kuomintang Central Executive Committee. This committee became large and did not meet often, so power passed into the hands of the Central Political Committee.

To this organ important measures were submitted for scrutiny; by this organ high officials of important government offices were appointed. For example, by it the chairman and the members of the State Council were appointed, as were the heads and vice-heads of the five Yüans.

In theory, the five Yüans are of equal status; in practice, the Executive Yüan has the commanding position. Under the Executive Yüan are a number of ministries and commissions. The other Yüans are the Legislative, the Judicial, the Examination Power, and the Control Power. The names of these Yüans suggest their functions. In addition there is the Military Commission, which is independent of the Executive Yüan itself.

This is but a brief sketch of the scheme of the Five Power Constitution. The scheme, though based upon the principles of the Five Power Constitution, did not manifest its spirit. It was too complex, and it was very difficult for the people to understand. Again, there was a good deal of overlapping, as the work was shared by a number of offices—government and party—and, moreover, it was not democratic, because no popular representation was provided.

Coming now to the wartime changes: as far as government proper is concerned, these have been few. The pre-war framework of the State Council, superimposed upon the five Yüans with the Military Commission assuming an equal position, has remained unaltered. However, immediately after the outbreak of the war in 1937, there were a few changes worth mentioning. There was, *inter alia*, the project for the establishment of a general headquarters. The idea was to supersede all organs of government, but this appeared to be too radical; consequently it was dropped. The Military Commission, however, was greatly extended and strengthened.

In 1938 the Executive Yüan likewise was overhauled. At first it had had nine ministries; after the outbreak of war the number was reduced to seven. Also, the Ministry of Labor was transferred to the Military Commission; the Ministry of Industry was reorganized as the Ministry of Economics, and the Ministry of Railways was merged with the Ministry of Communications. These changes were dictated by principles of efficiency and economy. Later three new ministries were added, namely, those of Agriculture and Forestry, of Food, and of Social Affairs.

The government of China is controlled by the Kuomintang, which, since 1927–28, has ruled most of the country largely through the instrumentality of the Central Political Committee. It is in the latter that the most important changes have taken place to make it better suited for conducting the war.

The Central Political Committee was a committee of the Central Executive Committee of the All China Congress. The membership became very large, since the members of the Central Executive Committee and those of the Central Control Committee had the right to be present at the meetings. In 1937 the Supreme Council of National Defense was established as a committee of the Central Political Committee and also as a substitute, in part, for that organ.

There are two differences between these organs:

first, the Supreme Council of National Defense is much smaller and, accordingly, better suited for conducting the war; second, the Supreme Council has emergency power of legislation, which the Central Political Committee did not have.

The Supreme Council of National Defense did some good work, but with the passage of time it was found that its powers were not extensive enough; moreover, the procedure of exercising these powers was not direct. In order to improve the situation, the Central Committee took action and the Supreme *Committee* of National Defense was organized to take the place of the Supreme *Council* of National Defense.

The Supreme Committee of National Defense differs from the Supreme Council of National Defense in three respects: first, in the Supreme Committee power is more concentrated in the hands of its chairman; second, the authority of the committee is extended to all departments, government as well as party; third, the Supreme Committee of National Defense can issue orders to all the subordinate departments of the five Yüans and the Military Commission.

The Supreme Committee of National Defense, however, is not a small organ, inasmuch as it consists of (1) members of the Standing Committee of the Central Executive Committee, (2) members of the Central Control Committee, (3) the heads and the vice-heads of the five Yüans, (4) the members of the Military Commission, and (5) other members nominated by the chairman of the committee with the consent of the Standing Committee of the Central Executive Committee.

Since the inauguration of the Supreme Committee of

National Defense, the Standing Committee of the Central Executive Committee still has its weekly meetings, but it confines its attention to party affairs. The Executive Yüan, which has to take orders from the Supreme Council, also meets weekly. The Military Commission must likewise respect the authority of the Supreme Committee of National Defense.

The Supreme Committee of National Defense has a secretariat whose secretary-general must be one of its members. The five committees on law, finance, economics, foreign affairs, and education, which formerly served the Central Political Committee, now serve the Supreme Committee of National Defense. The Supreme Committee also has the Planning Commission, which is headed by the chairman, i.e., Generalissimo Chiang, and the Control Committee, which is subdivided into two sections in charge of party and government.

Concerning post-war tendencies, it is believed that the constitutional regime will be introduced—and maybe before the end of the war, should the war continue for a considerable time longer.

Under the constitutional regime a constitution will be adopted, presumably, along the lines of the draft constitution of May 5, 1936. The Five Power system will probably remain—in part—because it was developed by the late Dr. Sun Yat-sen, who commanded the respect of most sections of the population. This system will be upheld by the Kuomintang. Another reason why the Five Power system will probably be retained is that it has been in operation for some years so that the people and the leaders are accustomed to its operation. This is a merit in itself. However, the new constitution must be something more than a Five Power system if it is to work well or, indeed, work at all. Under the Five Power system, the five Yüans will perhaps be of the same status—in which case they will possess no directing force; in case of conflict, there will be deadlock. In view of such defects, certain scholars and leaders are of the opinion that China should have a presidential system of government superimposed on the five Yüans.

With respect to national unity, the question is at times asked: "Is China a united nation as well as a United Nation?" To some, who think of the civil wars of recent years, and of the puppet governments set up by the Japanese military, China seems to be not completely united. To the Chinese student of government, however, these are but incidents in the mighty current of general political transformation and development of our gigantic nation. It is believed that most of the forces which have resulted in conflict and destruction have already been spent. The Chinese Quisling-puppets are only a handful of reactionary traitors who find their counterpart in the occupied regions in Europe. These must fall as soon as the Japanese have been defeated because they have no popular support.

China is a political entity with a bright future. History shows that China from the time of Ch'in Shih Huang Ti, in the third century B.C., to the present, for more than two thousand years, has been an essentially united nation. No social disturbances or changes of dynasties have ever succeeded in splitting the country permanently. This is no accident. There are many cohesive forces perennially working for unity.

In China there is no racial "minority problem." There

are five so-called racial groups. The Chinese are the dominant group, but they have seldom imposed discriminations or restrictions upon the other groups. The Manchus, having been overthrown as a ruling class, have not, since 1911–12, suffered persecution. Mohammedans, Chinese and non-Chinese, live in the four corners of the country and feel equally at home. The Mongols in the north and the Tibetans in the west have enjoyed a high degree of local autonomy. Members of the five groups enjoy essentially equal rights and opportunities. Having the spirit of tolerance among ourselves, we have no basically racial problem.

Nor do we have basic or permanent class distinctions. Since the unification of the empire, in the third century B.C., feudalism, though lingering on, vanished as a system never really to be revived. In China there are now no traces of aristocratic class rule. Buddhist priests are confined in the main to religious affairs, and they enjoy no special privileges. To this day scholars enjoy the highest social status, and children of humble families can rise to the top of society. Class distinction has little or no place with us. A classless society is conducive to harmonious development and democratic rule —and nothing less than democratic rule can satisfy the Chinese people.

China has rarely practiced religious persecution. Throughout the country there are Confucian temples, Buddhist temples, Mohammedan mosques, and Christian churches. Formerly Chinese scholars were generally considered to be Confucianists, although Confucianism, in the estimation of most people, can hardly be called a religion. The majority of the people accept the Buddhist creed, although there are many Mohammedans, and Christian churches also have many converts. These religious institutions preach different creeds, in general without interference and without molestation. Accordingly, religious conflicts and religious persecutions have not been common.

Language, customs, and habits all through China are basically similar. China is a great nation: great in culture, in population, and in territory. With perhaps one-fourth of the world's population and one-eighth of the global surface, there is one basic language which is spoken by at least 90 per cent of the population. There are, indeed, local dialects, but, thanks to the contemporary improvement of communication and of universal education, the "Mandarin" language can be understood in practically all parts of the country. Customs, habits, and ideas of life are basically the same from the borders of Mongolia to the South Sea Islands. The cohesive forces mentioned bind the constituent areas and peoples into a solid entity.

People may naturally ask: "Why is it that China, in spite of these numerous invaluable assets, has often had political and social disturbances?" Two reasons of many may be cited for these disturbances: first, contact with the West and, second, break with the past. The Chinese have traditions handed down for thousands of years. When westerners and Western institutions, learning, and ideas came into contact with the Chinese, we had to give up some traditions and take up some new institutions. Some traditions the people were unwilling and slow to give up; some of the new and alien Western institutions we were not at first prepared to operate properly. In the process of give-and-take, difficulties are bound to arise. Dissent without proper compromise leads to conflict. The second point is that the Japanese have been giving us trouble and have interfered in China's internal politics and external relations for two long generations. They have stood, and now stand, in our way of progress. However, we cannot blame others too severely; we ourselves have, indeed, lost many opportunities for improvement.

People may ask again: "How has China actually advanced in recent years?" For many years we did not have good government. The National Government has had its hands full since its establishment in 1928, first, against the Communists, supported at times by Russia, and recently against Japanese aggression. In a time of national crisis we cannot do as much as we would; but still we have done some things worth mentioning, for example, the problem of centralization of public finance. In the days of civil war among the war lords (1915 ff.), numerous sources of revenue of the central government passed into the hands of the provincial governments. The central government was at times unable to fulfil its obligations—not to speak of controlling the local authorities through the power of the purse. Since the establishment of the Nanking government in 1928, important sources of revenue have been allocated to the central government, the local authorities being assigned certain sources of revenue for their own needs. Centralization of finance means centralization of power in the hands of the central government. This may have been done at times without due regard for local needs; hence occasional stifling of local initiative.

A further instance: nationalization of China's armies. During the earlier years of the Republican revolution, leaders in various provinces recruited personal armies, and the commanders under Yuan Shih-k'ai, whom the latter sent into the provinces as military governors, kept troops as their private mercenaries. It was during this period (*ca.* 1915–28 and even later) that the war lords fought one another. After the establishment of the Nanking government, most of the war lords were put down, one after another. The Communists, after developing dangerous military power, were greatly reduced. Because of the national crisis a few divisions of the Communist troops were saved. Later, these took the lead in pledging themselves to fight the Japanese and encouraging the National Government to do likewise.

China's armies are now largely nationalized. This means that the generalissimo, at least in theory, controls all the armies. It may be hoped that some day these troops will be under the control of the National Assembly rather than under any one leader.

With respect to the problem of reconciliation of the political parties: of all the parties, the Kuomintang has been the biggest, and the dominant, one in China; the Communist party never enjoyed genuine, widespread, popular support; the other parties in existence can hardly be called parties, inasmuch as they are but handfuls of men of political ambitions. All the parties are now officially reconciled and pledged to support the government. All are given representation in the People's Political Council, and their delegates not infrequently voice the opinion of their respective parties. But how much they are actually reconciled and how much they have actually co-operated is a question which is difficult to answer. Minor conflicts have sometimes been heard of, but it may be hoped there will be no serious clash in the near future.

Owing to the ravages of war, people of various provinces have moved in mass migration from province to province. People in eastern China who never thought of seeing the northwest or the southwest have now settled down in Szechuan or in other provinces far from their original homes. War refugees from the different provinces have carried with them new ideas and new ways of life. With the ever greater scale of intermarriage and through the improvement of communications and universal education—also the introduction of conscription—the people of various provinces come into relatively or actually close contact with one another. Such contacts promote better understanding but may, at the same time, cause difficulties.

With regard to future prospects, from the developments mentioned it is evident that China, once free from outside interference, will be in a better position to develop into a modern nation. From bitter experience of war, people will become more conscious politically, and civil war will not be tolerated. On the other hand, the government will double its efforts toward a constructive program, and reactionary elements will have no chance of causing trouble. It is probable, therefore, that no civil war will come again.

With financial power and the armies under direct control, the central government will be greatly strengthened. A strong government will be in a better position to promote unity and to carry on constructive reforms. If the government receives popular support and also has a constructive program on its own side, it can indeed work wonders.

The next development to be expected is the inauguration of the constitutional regime. This will be an important factor in the maintenance of national unity. Establishment of the constitutional regime has for years been demanded by the people. The political parties, other than the Kuomintang, have had the same demand. So, when a constitutional regime is actually introduced, the people will support the government more consistently and the parties may be more nearly reconciled. Even on the part of the National Government itself, under the constitutional regime, officials will respect legality and will look after the interests of the people much more than they now do.

A few words must be said, also, about two more organizations, namely, the People's Political Council and the new District Code. The People's Political Council was created in 1938 by resolution of the All China Congress of the Kuomintang. The first council was convened on July 6, 1939. It had a membership of about two hundred, which can be divided into four categories: eighty members, representing provinces and municipalities, are to be nominated concurrently by the provincial government and the provincial party organization; six members, representing Mongolia and Tibet, are to be nominated by the Commission of Mongolian and Tibetan Affairs; and six representatives of overseas Chinese are to be nominated by the Commission on Overseas Affairs; and a hundred members represent cultural and economic associations. These are to be directly nominated by the Supreme Council of National Defense. Twice as many members are to be nominated as are to be chosen, and the final choice is to be in the hands of the Supreme Council of National Defense.

A few changes occurred in the second People's Political Council. The number of members was increased by forty. The provinces and the municipalities sent two members more than before, and the cultural and economic associations sent thirty-eight more members than previously.

As to the composition of the People's Political Council, the elected members gradually increased. Representatives of the Communists and other critics of the government have always been included. Of course, the council was still nominated by the Kuomintang.

As to the powers of the People's Political Council: first, the council is entitled to make proposals to the government and to ask the departments of government any question they like. The government departments, moreover, must give their annual reports to this body, and reports can be demanded at any time. Finally, it must be added, the People's Political Council has no power of compulsion—it is only advisory.

The new District Code was promulgated by the central government as a sign of preparation for the constitutional regime. According to law, each district in China must have as a legislature a District Council, the members of which are to be elected by the urban and the rural districts. A magistrate will be elected by the people as executive. That is the law. In practice, there are many differences. In some districts, for instance, the members of the District Council are mostly appointed by the provincial government on nomination of the magistrate. The magistrates, it is worthy of mention, are appointed temporarily.

And now to certain conclusions regarding what has been discussed. Concerning the machinery of government, it is clear and important to remember that, for the moment, China has a government by the Kuomintang. But the country is going to have a constitutional government after the war—or before the end of the war, perhaps, should the present struggle continue for any great length of time. Under the constitutional regime it is hoped to have a truly popular government, that is, a government by the people, of the people, and for the people. A truly responsible government is desired by the people—an efficient government, an intelligent government, and also an honest government.

In regard to national unity: China has been a united nation at various times in earlier centuries. In spite of differences and difficulties in recent years, the people and certain of their leaders have been working for national unity. The nation must be united at all costs, and there is excellent reason for belief that China will become a really united nation after this war.

As to trends toward democracy, may I say that China has enjoyed *social* democracy for hundreds of years. The purpose of the revolution of 1911 was to effect *political* democracy, of which the people as a whole and the leaders have not had much experience. But we have firm faith in the unity of democratic government, so it is believed we shall attain it by degrees.

PROBLEMS OF NUTRITION IN PRESENT-DAY CHINA

By Tsai Chiao

ONE cannot discuss the nutritional problems of China without taking into consideration the country's economic status and agricultural development and the health habits and education of the people. The country is vast, and there are few modern facilities for transportation to move the products of one province to the people of another. As a result, certain seasons will see an excess of a particular foodstuff in one region and a deficiency in another, while at other seasons the situation will be reversed. Nutrition varies, of course, with education, income, and mode of living, as well as with geographic location. Time does not allow me to go into the matter in detail, and I shall have to be content to speak in generalities with here and there a note as to some outstanding respect in which this or that region or class varies from the general pattern.

Recent studies by Chinese nutritional workers and food specialists show that, for the most part, Chinese diets are adequate in calories but deficient in animal protein, vitamins, and certain salts. Prior to 1937 the protein content of the average Chinese diet lay at the lower limit of the minimum recommended by the International Health Committee of the League of Nations—that is, it amounted to from 60 to 100 gm.

per day. Since the opening of the war this value has
dropped to between 50 and 80 gm. per day. It is of
great importance that 90 per cent of this very small
protein intake is from vegetable, rather than animal,
sources, because vegetable proteins are low in biological
value and must be taken in large amounts if they are to
substitute adequately for animal proteins. Recognizing
this fact, the Nutritional Committee of the Chinese
Medical Association recommended several years ago
that the protein in Chinese diets be raised well above
the minimum standards of the International Health
Committee of the League of Nations, but it has not
been possible to follow this recommendation. Statistical
data recently compiled by my colleagues in our department of biochemistry and public health in collaboration with workers in other colleges and government agencies show that in Kunming, Chengtu, and
Chungking between the years 1939 and 1941 the average college student consumed from 50 to 60 gm. of protein per day, of which from 5 to 10 gm. were of animal
origin. Soldiers in the recruiting camp near Chengtu,
and elsewhere in western China, fared no better than
the students and received animal food usually once, or
at most twice, a month. On this diet the soldiers
suffered from a good deal of xerophthalmia, trachoma,
skin infections, anemia, and parasitic infections. After
three months of adequate feeding, their mental performance, physical strength, and endurance were found
to be improved. As a result of such experiments it has
been recommended that soldiers' diets be improved.
It is not known how far the army has been able to follow

this advice. Hypoproteinemia and edema have been reported frequently in pregnant and lactating women in certain regions in northern China, and it is thought that the retarded growth and paleness of school children coming from poorer families may be explained on the basis of inadequate diets.

VITAMIN DEFICIENCY

Since an important source of fat-soluble vitamins is animal food, it may be assumed that the diets of poor people, students, and soldiers will be deficient in vitamins A, D, and E.

Vitamin A deficiency.—There is reason to believe that vitamin A deficiency is widespread in China. Theoretically it is possible to detect even a mild degree of deficiency by analysis of the blood or systematic studies of the rate of dark adaptation of the eye, but it has not yet been possible to undertake such examinations on a wide scale. For the time being we must depend upon an analysis of the diets themselves or the demonstration of clinical manifestations of the deficiency. These latter unfortunately are detectable only when the deficiency is of severe grade. The commonness among Chinese of chronic infectious diseases such as tuberculosis and trachoma, the high incidence of renal calculi and dental caries, and the slowness with which wounds commonly heal are thought to be manifestations of a vitamin A deficiency which has reduced resistance to infection.

Vitamin D.—In certain mountainous regions in northern China, including Manchuria, it is customary to confine children and pregnant women to the home, thus depriving them of sunshine. In these regions rickets and osteomalacia have been reported, but elsewhere in China vitamin D deficiency is not common.[1]

Vitamin B, deficiency.—This condition is encountered most commonly in eastern, central, and southern China, where polished rice forms an important part of the average diet. The introduction of unpolished rice into the diets of soldiers and school children has largely prevented the appearance of beriberi among these groups. However, the Chinese diet already contains an excess of cellulose and crude vegetable fiber, so that the addition of unpolished rice is likely to produce gastrointestinal disorders. Possibly improved methods of cooking would increase the digestibility of unpolished rice, or it may be necessary to substitute for it flour ground from the whole rice grain.

Beriberi is rarely seen in western China, probably because the people in this region use a rice that is incompletely polished and enjoy an abundance of fruit and vegetables.

Vitamin C deficiency.—Scurvy occurs in China only in poor families in certain localities in the north where citrus fruit is scarce in the late winter and spring. Recent studies on the ascorbic acid content of the blood and urine of school children in the western provinces suggest that there, as well as in other parts of the country, there may be mild subclinical vitamin C deficiency during the spring when fruits are scarce and expensive.

---

[1] This opinion, widely held, may be fallacious. Without the aid of X-rays, rickets is likely to go undetected. As yet X-rays have been available to only an extremely insignificant number of Chinese children even in the port cities, to say nothing of rural districts.

VOICES FROM UNOCCUPIED CHINA

MINERAL DEFICIENCIES AND IMBALANCE

Calcium.—Observers in Szechuan have reported a high level of calcium in the diet. Elsewhere, however, the calcium content of the ordinary diet is low. In northern Shansi, where rickets and osteomalacia are prevalent, the diet is said to be low not only in calcium but also in vitamin D.

Iodine deficiency.—Iodine deficiency has been reported at various places in northern China as well as in the southwestern provinces; but there are no recognized endemic goiter areas, and, as yet, general preventive measures have not been adopted.

Excessive fluoride intake.—Mottled dental enamel caused by an excessive amount of fluoride in drinking water and in certain varieties of tea has been reported in western Chekiang, northern Fukien, and in certain villages in Sikang. In northern Kweichow there have been reported cases of osteopetrosis and deformity of the spine which were thought to be the result of fluoride intoxication. It will require careful investigation to establish whether or not there is a relationship between these skeletal lesions and the amount of fluoride in the diet.

Barium poisoning.—In Kiating, which lies about one hundred kilometers southwest of Chengtu, there is an endemic disease called "Kiating paralysis." This is characterized by a sudden onset of paralysis of the extremities, followed by paralysis of the facial muscles, and later of the muscles of the chest. Some of the patients recover spontaneously after a few days; others die from paralysis of the muscles of respiration. It has been reported that intravenous injection of potassium citrate is beneficial and frequently relieves the symptoms promptly.

It has been shown conclusively that the table salt used in this region contains a good deal of barium as an impurity, and the suggestion has been made that the paralysis is a manifestation of barium poisoning. Proof of this awaits the opportunity to analyze the blood of these patients for barium. In the meantime the government has taken the precaution of prohibiting the sale of table salt that is excessively contaminated with barium.

RELATIONSHIP OF NUTRITION TO OTHER FACTORS IN CHINESE LIFE

If nutrition in China is to be improved, there must simultaneously be improved the general economy, the output of agricultural products, and the health education of the people. The serious deficiency of animal protein in the diets of soldiers, students, and the poor is obviously the result of economic factors. Previous to the onset of military operations in 1937, the *annual* income of the average Chinese farmer was about $50, Chinese currency. This amount of money will not purchase sufficient food for the maintenance of life. At present the situation has improved for farmers in western China because they can now sell their surplus of food at higher prices; but farmers in the Japanese-occupied areas are worse off than they previously were, because their surplus products are taken from them by the enemy. Until the economic level can be raised in China, the fundamental problems of nutrition will remain largely unsolved.

Agriculture.—In the limited time at my disposal I am able to sketch only the merest outline of the ways in which Chinese agriculture must be improved if the problems of malnutrition in our country are to be solved.

Animal husbandry and dairy products.—There is little or no dairying in China at present. In Chungking and in Chengtu it is difficult to buy butter or cheese at any price, while the little milk that is available sells for $12, Chinese, a pint, which is the approximate equivalent of 60 cents in American money. If it were possible to provide China with an adequate amount of inexpensive milk, butter, and cheese, the principal nutritional problem would at once be solved. Of course, it is economically unsound to convert cultivated land into ranches, but this would be unnecessary, inasmuch as there are vast uncultivated areas scattered throughout the western provinces of China, particularly in northern Szechuan, Sikang, Kansu, Chinghai, and Sinkiang, which, according to a recent survey by the Minister of Agriculture and Forestry, are suitable for animal husbandry. If these uncultivated areas can be put to full use for the raising of beef cattle and dairy herds, there will be no lack of dairy products and beef in China. Such large-scale development will, of course, take time and will have to go hand in hand with the development of transportation, large-scale facilities for the canning, packing, and storage of foods, and particularly the development of a system of public health and veterinary medicine. The government bureau of veterinary medicine has made a beginning, but a very great deal of work remains to be done. For example, infections still cause the loss of thousands of pigs and chickens in Szechuan alone each year.

Meanwhile, however, a great deal could be accomplished by the establishment of large numbers of small dairies throughout the country. The present high price of milk and other dairy products is a stimulant to such development, particularly in suburban regions, but development is slow because, in part, of the lack of milch cows. Scientific selection and breeding would probably increase the yield of milk from buffaloes and goats, which at present are used to a limited extent and without much profit because of the smallness of the yield.

Fish.—Fish nurseries, which have long flourished in the central and southern sections of the country, are now being introduced into the western provinces. Sea fishing is important because of the great length of coast line. When this has been developed, along with scientific methods for the storing and shipping of fish, an important step will have been taken toward increasing the protein in Chinese diets.

Improved storage, packaging, transportation, and marketing.—In Szechuan millions of oranges and apples are wasted annually because of insect infestation and lack of adequate storage and packing facilities. Eggs used to be produced in enormous quantities in eastern and central China—but even before the war they were largely unavailable for Chinese diets because, for the most part, they were diverted into the export trade. Now that these regions are under Japanese domination, it is safe to assume that fewer eggs are available for consumption by Chinese. Before the war the writer publicly protested the wholesale exportation of eggs in

the hope of decreasing the price and increasing the supply available for the poor, but the protests received
scant attention by government officials of that period,
who were more concerned with the revenue of the
country than with the nutrition of the people.

Health education.—By no means least important in
the problem of improving the nutrition of the Chinese
is the need for improved and enlarged public health
education. The people must be given an elementary
knowledge of nutrition and a demonstration of its importance in the health, in the ability to work effectively,
and in the general well-being and happiness of the race.
By this means our countrymen may learn to choose and
prepare foods more intelligently. Millions of families,
particularly in rural districts, must be taught to dis-
card their traditional, or even superstitious, dislike of
milk, butter, and meat. They must be taught that
drying and boiling largely destroys vitamin C in vegetables and fruit, that polishing removes vitamin B from
rice, and that soybeans, which are produced in vast
quantities in China, are extremely nourishing. Few
Chinese use sugar regularly in their diets. Many
Chinese, particularly in the interior, live for long
periods on diets deficient in proteins and fat and then,
occasionally, indulge in feasts containing an excess of
fat and proteins. This frequently causes indigestion
and a loss of important foodstuffs that might better
have been spread over days and weeks instead of concentrated in a single meal.

There are innumerable other ways in which our
people need health education relative to diet. A beginning has been made among school children, and this,

of course, should be encouraged; but about 60 per cent of the Chinese are illiterate and can be reached only by visual education in such forms as moving pictures and posters or by broadcasting. The Ministry of Education, the National Health Administration, and numerous provincial educational and health bureaus have begun such work, but the extent is relatively small because of limited equipment and funds. In Szechuan the provincial Commission of Education has been experimenting with moving pictures and has obtained some favorable results. Public health nurses are carrying the story of nutrition to individual families—but here, too, the work is still on an extremely limited scale.

CONCLUSIONS

As indicated above, the problem of nutrition in China is closely linked with the economic, agricultural, and industrial development of the country and the health education of the people. It can be solved only by simultaneous progress along all these lines, which will require effort on the part of all Chinese directly concerned and of many others who are so fortunately situated as not to be directly involved in starvation and malnutrition.

THE MODERN PUBLIC HEALTH MOVE-
MENT IN CHINA

By C. K. CHU

THE public health movement in China is less than twenty years old, but experimentation has been so vigorous and progress so rapid that, except for the interruption of war, we should now be well on the way toward a widespread system adapted to the peculiar needs of our people and our country.

Public health service began in China in 1925 when the Peking Health Demonstration Station was established under the joint auspices of the Peking Union Medical College and the police department of the metropolis of Peking. Dr. John B. Grant, who at that time was professor of public health and hygiene in the Peking Union Medical College, founded the station; and practically all of the public health leaders in China today have been connected with it at one time or another.

When the National Government was established in Nanking in 1928, a Ministry of Health was set up with Dr. J. Heng Liu as vice-minister and later as minister. In 1930 the Ministry of Health was reorganized as the National Health Administration with Dr. Liu as director-general, and at about the same time the Central Field Health Station was established under the National Economic Council of the central government. The functions of the National Health Administration are administrative, whereas the Central Field Health Station serves as a technical agency for the demonstration of various phases of public health service.

The period 1928-37, immediately prior to the outbreak of the present Sino-Japanese war, was a golden era in public health work in China. During these nine years it was possible to demonstrate the curative and preventive possibilities of modern medicine, including laboratory services, and to bring to government administrators a realization of the importance of public work as a governmental function.

At Nanking there were established the Central Hospital as a demonstration of modern curative medicine and the Central Field Health Station as a demonstration of health laboratory and research service. The Commission on Medical Education was organized under the joint auspices of the Ministry of Education and the National Health Administration and began a coordinated program of medical education. A Public Health Personnel Training Institute was set up under the National Health Administration, and systems of rural, or *hsien*, health service were inaugurated in Ting-hsien, Kiaochiao, Chiangning, and other rural places.

With the beginning of war in July, 1937, this public health program was interfered with and most of its achievements in Nanking were destroyed. After the evacuation of Nanking at the end of 1937, practically all national and provincial public health workers had to turn to the relief of wounded soldiers and refugees.

By 1939 the Army Medical Service and the Chinese Red Cross had been able to organize medical services to meet the emergency, and the National Health Administration gradually resumed its regular public health functions. The public health problems of wartime China are quite different from those of peacetime, however. The war, together with a westward movement of population, created a situation favorable to the outbreak of epidemics, so the first concern of the National Health Administration had to be the control of epidemic diseases. Among infectious diseases occurring in epidemic form, plague and cholera were the most serious.

Plague, which had been endemic in a few isolated areas in Manchuria, Fukien, and Yünnan, became epidemic between July, 1940, and December, 1942, in certain parts of Chekiang, Fukien, Kwangtung, Kiangsi, Hunan, and Suiyuan, causing numerous deaths.

From 1938 to 1940, there were serious cholera epidemics, the disease spreading throughout the fifteen provinces in Free China with a total of about fifty thousand cases for the three years.[1] Malaria also constitutes a serious problem in Free China, being particularly prevalent in the provinces of Yünnan, Kweichow, and Kwangsi, where whole villages have been depopulated by the disease. The subtertian type is the commonest, the most serious, and has the highest

[1] On this Dr. Liu commented a few minutes later: "Dr. Chu mentions ten thousand cases in three years. He probably means ten thousand *reported* cases. I am sure that the actual number would be much larger than that. But even if the figure is one hundred thousand it is not bad. In six years of fighting under terrible conditions, an epidemic of cholera could be so bad in a country like China that millions would die from it. We are fortunate that these epidemics have not been worse than they were. Quite possibly it is the work of the National Health Administration that has limited them. As soon as they hear reports of a number of cases in a locality, the Health Service people go there and start large campaigns of inoculations against cholera. I think we must conclude that cholera immunization is effective."

mortality. Relapsing fever and typhus fever constitute serious problems, particularly in the north-western provinces. Tuberculosis has increased notably in recent years, owing to general deficiencies in diet and nutrition. Possibly the incidence of tuberculosis among college and high-school students may be something more than 5 per cent of the total population.[2] The situation has become acute, and the government health authorities, realizing this, have induced the National Government and the city government of Chungking to appropriate this year [1943] a rather large sum of money for the establishment of tuberculosis sanatoriums. But the problem is so enormous that even with this appropriation it may not be possible for us to start anything of great importance. In the first place, we haven't enough specialists on tuberculosis, and, in the second place, we can scarcely hope to provide enough sanatorium beds. We now have a small sanatorium in Chungking. Its sixty beds are always full, with a waiting list booked six or eight months ahead. A sanitorium for the city of Chungking alone should have a capacity of not less than five hundred beds, whereas our present appropriation can support less than one hundred. And that is but one phase of the difficulty.

To help the local health authorities in preventing, or controlling, epidemic diseases, the National Health Administration in 1938 organized a Wei-Shen-Shu

[2] Commenting on living conditions in the refugee educational institutions in Free China, Dr. Chiao Tsai observed: "The living quarters for college students are certainly very bad because many of these schools were moved to the interior of China from the occupied area and they put up temporary buildings which are absolutely crowded with students. They are sleeping in double-deck beds, and I think a room of this size [34 × 30 ft.] may accommodate forty or fifty students."

Anti-epidemic Corps. The corps, with its four geographical divisions in Szechuan, Hunan, Kwangsi, and Chekiang, now has a total of twenty-four units, and all of them are mobile, so that they can be dispatched to areas where epidemics break out. The importance of the work of the Anti-epidemic Corps can be illustrated by the following incident of control. In 1939 a cholera epidemic broke out in Kweiyang, Kweichow, and a total of seventeen hundred cases was reported. It lasted from June 2 to September 12, 1938. As soon as we received the report of the first case, we started concurrently a mass-immunization campaign and a water-purification campaign. The curve of that epidemic reached its peak on August 1 and declined sharply thereafter. Of the several factors responsible for this break, two are outstanding. First, our immunization campaign had reached 65 per cent of the total population of the city by July 15; second, one week before August 1 we closed down twelve presumably infected public wells. Basing our action upon such experience, we instructed the provincial health officers to start a cholera immunization campaign by April 1, each year, so that by the middle of June from 30 to 40 per cent of the population would be immunized. Concurrently, a strict system of water purification was to be started whenever there were outbreaks of cholera in the neighboring cities. This program of control seems to have succeeded in preventing the outbreak of cholera epidemics in Kweiyang in the subsequent years.

The second phase of public health work in wartime China is the initiation of public health services. Both the national and the local governmental authorities are keenly aware of the importance of this work. Whenever a governor of a province has been appointed, he has usually called on the director of the National Health Administration for assistance and for the recommendation of a person suitable for appointment as provincial health commissioner. Similarly, when a *hsien* (county) magistrate is appointed, he usually asks the provincial health commissioner to recommend a health officer and to assist in setting up a *hsien* health service. In spite of the war, there have been developed in Free China during the last three or four years 15 provincial health administrations, 783 *hsien* health centers, and 57 highway health stations, the latter operating under the National Health Administration.

Faced with wartime limitations of facilities and personnel, it has been difficult to accomplish this rapid expansion of public health services without seriously affecting the quality of the work. In an effort to maintain and improve this quality, the National Institute of Health was established in April, 1941, by amalgamating the Central Field Health Station and the Public Health Personnel Training Institute. The National Institute of Health, operating under the National Health Administration, has research, planning, and the training of senior public health technical personnel as its chief responsibilities.

Steps are being taken to carry out extensive epidemiological surveys of the more common communicable diseases; to make dietary and nutritional surveys; and to work out a satisfactory system of rural water supply and sewage disposal, as well as standard laboratory methods. In addition, preventive dentistry and systems of urban and rural health services are being demonstrated in the neighborhood of Chungking.

China is not only fighting an antiaggression war; it is also carrying out a program of national reconstruction. Public health work has been recognized by the government as playing an important part in national reconstruction. Because of the immensity of its rural population, the magnitude of its public health problems, and the extreme shortage of technical personnel, China finds that none of the forms of public health service that has been developed in America or Europe is exactly suited to its needs.

For a population roughly estimated at 450,000,000 there are registered under the National Health Administration only 12,018 doctors; 5,796 nurses; 5,003 midwives; 793 pharmacists; and 322 dentists. In terms of population, there is one modern-trained doctor for 37,500 people! Of the "old-style" doctors, who are unregistered but practice, nevertheless, there are about 600,000. Most of the modern scientifically trained doctors are located in the large cities.

There are 30 medical schools in China, but they graduate annually less than 500 doctors. The annual production of nurses, midwives, pharmacists, and dentists is still less.

Infant mortality is about 200 per 1,000 live births, and the crude death rate is about 30 per 1,000. About 42 per cent of the annual deaths are due to preventable communicable diseases. When I first came to the United States, it was suggested to me that some kind of birth control ought to be started in China, but at present I do not think this can be done. Even in the United States you have met difficulties, I believe, and have had to change your term from "birth control" to "parenthood education" or "child spacing."

If we are able to expand our health service to the extent of making medical care available to our rural population, then incidentally and unobtrusively we may be able to introduce child spacing as a phase of maternal and child health. It is my personal opinion that it would be a waste of time to talk about birth control in China at present.

To solve the public health problems in China, the National Health Administration has initiated a system of organized state medical service, in which both curative and preventive medicine will be applied hand in hand. This service will be graded into different types according to the needs, and it will be distributed systematically so as to make it available to the masses of people in China. This system is known as "state medicine."

Medical research, education, and service are to be co-ordinated by means of commissions established under the joint auspices of the Ministry of Education and the National Health Administration. The medical and public health service are of three types: national, provincial, and *hsien*. The National Health Administration, with its subsidiary organizations, constitutes the National Medical and Public Health Authority.

For each province there is a Provincial Health Administration under which there are technical institutions, such as provincial hospitals, provincial public health laboratories, and provincial commissions on health education. For each municipality, or *hsien*, there is a municipal department or a *hsien* health center. This consists—or, it is hoped, eventually will consist—of a hospital with from fifty to a hundred beds, a clinic, and a public health service.

It is planned that, for each rural district of from fifty to one hundred thousand inhabitants, there will be a rural health subcenter consisting of an emergency ward, a clinic, and a public health supervisory service. For each market town of from 5,000 to 10,000 population it is hoped that there will be a rural health station to be staffed by a nurse and a midwife, who will treat simple ailments, carry on antenatal and delivery services, provide school health and health education service and inoculations, and supervise sanitation.

We have not encountered much suspicion among rural people, but, of course, we approach them as tactfully as possible. The first thing we do when we get to a rural area is to open a clinic that gives free medical service. Our maternal and child health service usually is welcomed by rural communities and frequently the story goes like this.

A country woman has a difficult labor that lasts for two or three days, and it becomes evident that the local old-fashioned midwives will not be able to get the baby out. At midnight relatives knock at the door of our health station asking our aid, and if our doctor delivers that baby safely by the next day his reputation is secure. Farmers tell one another: "Now, here is a doctor who can turn a dead baby into a living baby." So far our rural health service has been quite successful.

It is our hope that in the post-war period we may be able to train sufficient technical personnel so that every village of from 500 to 1,000 population may have public health workers qualified to vaccinate for smallpox, render first aid, and report births and deaths.

THE ORIGIN AND DEVELOPMENT OF PUBLIC HEALTH SERVICE IN CHINA

By J. Heng Liu

D R. CHU has told you about my relationship to the development of public health service in China. I started out to be a surgeon, and after returning from America to China in 1915 I practiced surgery and taught it until about 1922 or 1923, when I was asked to become the superintendent of the (Rockefeller) Peking Union Medical College hospital. It was while I was superintendent of that hospital that I became interested in public health work.

I remember one experience in particular. I was sitting in my office when a group of Peking merchants came to see me. They said that their native village, which lay twenty-five or thirty miles from Peking, had a serious problem. It was a small village of four or five hundred families and for the preceding three or four years every one of the babies born there had died within ten days of birth. They wanted me, as superintendent of the hospital, to tell them what to do about it.

Never had a question like that been put to me; but fortunately it occurred to me that the condition might be tetanus of the newborn, which is as much an infectious or contagious disease as is scarlet fever or measles. It is a disease spread by midwives from mother to mother and to the babies. Perhaps every baby was being infected with tetanus.

At that time the Peking Public Health Station, which Dr. Chu has mentioned, had just been established. We arranged to send a woman doctor and a nurse to the village, and we investigated. True enough, it was tetanus neonatorum. The doctor and the nurse got the midwives together (they are not professional midwives but just grandmothers, old ladies who handle the deliveries) and gave them lessons on how to wash their hands, how to clean up, and how to boil the few utensils and instruments which they used. The next babies, and practically all the babies that were born afterward, were all right. We had put a stop to the epidemic. Our work was effective.

In a country like the United States you don't hear of these epidemics, not an epidemic of so many cases of tetanus neonatorum. And if you did—well, you have a public health service.

At that time in China (that was under the old Peking government which had no public health service) nothing was done for the people in the line of public health. That taught me a lesson. I said: "Now if I continue as a surgeon, of course I can teach medical students to become surgeons also; but *now* it is about time for somebody to begin to organize a public health service in China."

So I got very much interested in this Public Health Station in Peking. It was a very small demonstration station in one part of the city, but it was there that a few men were trained to do public health work. Then when the Nanking government was established in 1928 and the Ministry of Health was included in the setup of the new government and I was asked to go to Nanking to be the technical vice-minister of the new ministry, I very gladly went.

I gave up surgery for good—well, I did a little surgery for the first two or three years I was in Nanking, but for practical purposes I changed my profession from that of a surgeon to that of a public health official. It was during the nine years that I spent in Nanking that I set up the beginnings of the Chinese Public Health Service.

In addition to the Ministry of Health, which was later changed to the National Health Administration, we set up the Central Field Health Station. That was the technical department of the Public Health Administration. I might tell you a little concerning the beginnings, that is, the establishment of the Central Field Health Station.

In the first place, I may say, I do not like the name. It was given not by us in China but by a committee of experts called together by the Health Section of the League of Nations in Geneva. At that time, at the beginning of this public health development, I called for the assistance and collaboration of the Health Section of the League of Nations. They felt it was so important an undertaking that we could not afford to make mistakes in the organization of the new health service, so the Health Section of the League of Nations called the leading public health experts in the countries of Europe and they helped me to organize, or put on paper the organization of, this new service, which they thought had better be called the Central Field Health Station. It is a clumsy name, and I am glad Dr. Chu, since he took it over, has changed it to the National Institute of Health.

In this health station there are services on sanitary engineering and sanitation; on maternal and child health; on chemistry and pharmacology; on epidemiology, parasitology, and malariology; on vital statistics; on school health and health education; on industrial hygiene; on rural public health, and so forth—altogether, nine departments.

We had nothing at the beginning, but we started our buildings. At that time we built the central hospital, of which I was the promoter and also the first superintendent.

We were making big strides during the first nine years, and the interruption by the war in 1937 was a terrible blow to the work. It stopped everything for a couple of years. We took some of the equipment with us, but most of it was left in Nanking and now is in the hands of the Japanese. But, anyway, we had laid the foundations of the public health service of China, and Dr. Chu has reported to you on how the service has progressed in spite of the war, particularly the program on social medicine which we started in several places as a demonstration. Now it has grown until of 1,200 *hsiens*, or counties, in Free China today, 783 have their own health centers.

These centers in country places are not very much. If you should visit one of them, you would see a building with a big sign, "The Public Health Station"; but, if you walked in, you would find in some of them a few doctors, in others only one or two doctors, and, maybe, three or four or one or two nurses. But, anyway, every place has its own health department, and, in spite of limited personnel and budget and limited medical supplies, they are able to do a great deal of excellent work.

So much for the public health service. Next, for a brief consideration of the army medical service. Dr. Chu has reported to you the figures of medical personnel. The figures sound very bad, but actually they are worse. He talks about the registration of 12,018 doctors. That is the total number of doctors who have been registered since I started the registration of modern doctors in 1929, almost fifteen years ago. Now, in fifteen years, a number must have died, and I think Dr. Chu hasn't subtracted the number of deaths. Surely, with the war in addition to the ordinary mortality rate, 2,000 must have died, so I would put the number of doctors in China at about 10,000.

Then perhaps half, maybe a little less than half, are now in Occupied China. Most of the doctors were in the larger cities, and the larger cities are now all in Japanese-occupied territory. Most of these doctors, or at least many of them, have not been able to get out, so that in cities such as Peking, Hankow, Shanghai, Tientsin, Canton, and other large cities, many of the doctors still remain. In Free China we probably do not have more than 5,000 or 6,000 doctors.

The public health service and the provincial health services employ, roughly, 2,000 doctors, and there are about 30 medical colleges that must have a few hundred doctors on their staffs.

The Chinese army has something like five or six million men in the field and requires 30,000 medical officers. Your American army, up until last year, had 35,000 doctors, and now the number is over 40,000. Our problem is: How can we get 30,000 medical officers with only 3,000–4,000 available doctors? Of course, the answer is that most of them won't be doctors. We do have 30,000 medical officers, but except for 2,000 (about 7 per cent) they are not graduates of medical colleges and can serve only as medical aids.

In this country you have nurses' aids who are working in your hospitals because you haven't enough nurses to go around. In China we face the same problem with doctors and solve it in the same way. The junior medical officers in our army are not doctors at all; they are aids who have had very simple and short courses of training. They are able to do a first-aid dressing; they know a few things about stopping hemorrhages; they know a few essentials about antisepsis and asepsis; they know how to put a splint on a fracture. There are a few drugs that they can prescribe and administer to the wounded. For six years the Chinese army has been getting along that way.[1]

We have established schools for the training of aids or

[1] Questioned on the type of immunization given in the Chinese armies, Dr. Liu replied: "Our stocks of tetanus antitoxin are not large enough to allow giving a dose to every wounded man. During the first few months of fighting around Shanghai we had two or three hundred thousand wounded over a period of three or four months, and were able to give antitoxin to almost all of them; but since Nanking has been lost and our armies have retreated to the interior there hasn't been much intensive fighting. It is true that our hospitals are always full of wounded, but we no longer receive new cases in large numbers. In addition to this, the fighting front is now very long, and the fighting itself is largely of the guerilla type. Much of it goes on behind the Japanese lines so that transport of all sorts is difficult—particularly the transport of medical supplies, doctors, and the wounded.

"I have not received recent specific information from Chungking relative to tetanus, but our medical statistics are nothing to boast about, and even medical assistants. The one which is probably best known in this country is the one organized and directed by Dr. Robert Lim, one of our leading physiologists. Dr. Lim calls it the Emergency Medical Services Training School, and he has trained several thousand medical assistants, giving them a few months' training in elementary courses in the medical sciences and in elementary surgery. There are, moreover, short courses on sanitation, nursing, and laboratory technique. Dr. Lim's technicians will probably remain as junior medical officers in the army; I do not think the National Health Administration will ever grant them licenses to practice medicine. At the same time, Dr. Lim is starting a new program in his school, a course which he calls a "three-grade" training. He takes some of the younger medical aids, gives them two years' training, and then sends them back to the army for a period of one or two years. Later they return for two more years of study, followed by another period in the army and, finally, after a third two-year period in Dr. Lim's school, they qualify as doctors.

There is an Army Medical College under the Ministry of War, but it turns out only 50 or 60 graduates a year. Recent classes have been larger, but, I am sure, there are not more than 100 in a class.

---

if I had figures it isn't likely that they would be accurate enough to allow drawing any conclusions.

"Venereal disease is a pretty serious problem in the Chinese army, and our commanders do not believe in prophylaxis. Many of them feel that a soldier shouldn't expose himself to infection. The Army Medical Administration has tried to introduce venereal prophylaxis, but usually it brings so much discussion, on moral and other grounds, that it has always been turned down. The rate of venereal disease is pretty high."

It has been mentioned that we have about 30 medical colleges but that the total number of graduates is not over 500 a year. You will probably ask why the classes aren't larger. In the first place, with two or three exceptions, all the medical colleges had to be moved from one city to another some two or three times before they settled down, and they were moved in such a hurry that most of their equipment was lost. The teachers and the students went, but only a few portable things that were easily carried went with them.

At first, some replacements could be purchased through Hongkong, or through Indo-China, or over the Burma Road; but during the last two years very little equipment and few books or journals have been sent in. With the limited equipment it is difficult to enlarge the classes or to increase the number of schools.

Most of you know about the American Bureau for Medical Aid to China which operates as an agency of United China Relief. Even before Pearl Harbor, when the United States was still neutral, this bureau was doing a great deal to help the Chinese medical program, particularly at Dr. Robert Lim's school—the school for the training of medical assistants. Now a large part of the budget of the American Bureau for Medical Aid to China is being spent on that very useful purpose.

The American Bureau helps also in the program of the National Health Administration, but transportation is a difficult problem. Before Pearl Harbor it was possible to send in equipment and supplies; at present it is almost impossible to send anything. Some of the medical supplies used by the Chinese army are provided by the

Lend-Lease Administration or through the Lend-Lease Administration from the War Department in Washington; but transportation facilities are so limited that we are not asking for much, and, of the little we do receive, a considerable portion is held up by the bottleneck in India. Steamers are still running between the United States and India, steamers that can carry many tons, but from India to China goods have to go by airplane.

The American Red Cross helps by giving certain medical supplies for the civilian needs of China, but it, too, has transport troubles; and I understand that three-quarters of a million dollars' worth of Red Cross medical supplies have been in India for a year or more and cannot be delivered to China. The new Red Cross representative in China has finally managed to send in some two hundred tons, but that is not a very large quantity.

China is really in a bad way for medical supplies. Sulfa drugs which you buy here for a few cents cost up to $50, Chinese (U.S., $2.50), a tablet. A small bottle of cod-liver oil or halibut-liver oil, enough for a baby for a month or two, costs $1,200 (U.S., $60). A tablet of quinine is worth several dollars. The rate of exchange is now 20:1—that is, $1.00 Chinese is worth about 5 cents in American money. Inflation is not caused solely by scarcity. Food prices have gone up fifty to a hundred times since the war began in 1937, so that a pound of rice which used to cost 10 cents now sells for $5.00. Imported goods and scarce goods, such as drugs and medicines, bring from several hundred to several thousand times their pre-war price. Russia is not able to substitute for the Burma Road. The route from Russia is too long and too tedious. Even after goods imported from Russia arrive at the border, there is still a long haul by truck to the interior of China; and when I left China almost a year ago gasoline sold for $700 (U.S., $35) a gallon, and a tire cost $10,000 (U.S., $500).

SOME SOCIAL PROBLEMS
OF FREE CHINA[1]

By FEI HSIAO-T'UNG

A SURVEY of population in China reveals its extremely uneven distribution. Southwestern China, especially Yünnan, is very thinly populated; but the small figure of the average density does not mean that in that region the people have plenty of land to live on. Nearly 90 per cent of the land in Yünnan, according to Cressey's *Geographical Foundations of China*, is made up of uncultivable mountain ranges. Offering little help to the livelihood of the people, the rough surface serves mainly as a barrier to communication.

Settlements are found in the scattered and small valleys. Congested and crowded villages in the oval flat bottoms of valleys present a scene which always reminds me of my native land around Lake Tai, in Kiangsu Province, in the Yangtze Valley. The density of population around Kunming is estimated by the author of an article reprinted in *Agrarian China* as 400 per square mile. If we refine our statistics by taking only cultivated land into consideration, the density of population in Yünnan will not be much lower than that in Kiangsu, which is 896.

For at least five centuries immigrants from various

[1] The region mainly discussed is within one hundred kilometers of Kunming, provincial capital of Yünnan, the province "South of the Clouds."

parts of China have flowed into the frontier provinces and settled themselves in the fertile valleys. Carried with them was the traditional ideology of filial prosperity—of having many sons—which, in Yünnan, must have been as effective as elsewhere in China to bring up the size of the population in a short period to the saturation point.

The limited lands in the valleys are surrounded by mountains and soon became too small to give full employment to the settlers. However fertile the land may be, under the ever increasing burden of population it will eventually be hard to provide decent standards of living. At present the frontier provinces constitute no exception to the generalization made by Professor Tawney that "the population of China is too large to be supported by existing resources."

Having studied conditions in several villages in Yünnan, I have been deeply impressed by the inadequacy of the land for giving full employment to the peasants. Idle hands are numerous, even during the busy period of farming. According to my analysis, a small fraction of the existing labor supply is sufficient to carry on the agricultural work. According to the previously mentioned article in *Agrarian China*, it is estimated that only about 26–36 per cent of the potential labor power is actually employed in that region. But, since there are limited opportunities for profitable employment in labor other than agricultural, the peasants have to depend mainly on land for their living.

The existence of a huge potential labor force in the villages in Yünnan has resulted in extremely low payment of farm workers. In 1938, for instance, the wage for a farm worker in the village I investigated was 10 cents silver per day with food. But the period for which a laborer could find farm work lasted only about 140 days a year. When he was not hired for farm work, he had to provide his own food, which cost him 8 cents a day in 1938. Thus, his total income from hiring out his labor in farm work would not be sufficient to maintain himself alone during the long period of unemployment. It was necessary for him to seek subsidiary jobs, such as carrying salt, and to cut down expenses by taking a poor quality of food.

From his hand-to-mouth income, the laborer could not hope to have enough savings to start family life without an intensely hard struggle. If he were fortunate enough to marry, his industrious wife could not earn more than half his income, since the wage for female workers was only 5 cents a day. The burden of a family with children would be too heavy to maintain health in the already undernourished laborers.

Cheap labor blocks technical development. Farm animals are few because they are more expensive than human labor. In the village I investigated there are only nineteen out of one hundred and twenty-two households which raise oxen for farming. Most of the farm work is done with extremely simple tools or, indeed, without any sort of implements; for instance, weeding is literally done by hand.

Under these conditions farm work means simply physical torture. Though so much human labor is used in farming, the individual plots of land are still too small to give full employment to the villagers. In spite of low wages, hard work, and limited employment, the laborers who have no land or have too little land must hire themselves out to avoid starvation.

Landowners, with cheap labor at their command, can easily avoid toiling on the farms by hiring laborers to do the work for them. The owners find managing their farms by hiring short-term workers more profitable than renting their farms to tenants. Pushed aloof from taking part in actual work on the farm, they become a leisure class. It is true that they would obtain a better income if they would work on their farms themselves, since they do not use their energy and time that has been freed from farm work for other productive work, but this they do not take into consideration. The traditional attitude of despising manual labor supports the system. We may recall the saying of the Manchus: "Those who earn their living by labor are destined to be ruled."

Not only are laborers poorly paid, they are lowly considered. One of the landowners in the village laughed heartily when I suggested to him that he should take up the work himself. He said: "My dear friend, you will not find anyone who possesses 'face' who will work on a farm."

This retiring, and easily satisfied, mode of life may appear to be untenable in an acquisitive society, but it seems that the landowners know the secret of enjoyment which is to be obtained from non-seeking of the fruits of self-exploitation. To praise or to condemn their attitude is not our present concern. What I wish to emphasize is that this attitude should be taken into account as a mental adjustment to a completed system working on a limited resource and stable technology.

The dichotomy of leisure and toil in the traditional

structure is not a fixed formation but a dynamic equilibrium. Sacrificing income and indulging in nonproductive pursuits render the leisure class economically vulnerable, especially so when its members are tempted to form the habit of opium smoking. Any stroke of misfortune then sends them down into the poorer classes and forces them to suffer the hard toil of life.

Even for a well-protected small owner there is always a tendency to go to the bottom when his holdings are divided among his sons. The ideology of filial prosperity serves as a check against perpetuation of the leisure class.

Then, we may ask, how can the peasant climb up from the landless to the landowner class, and from the small-owner to the large-owner class? I have already indicated the grave prospects for poor laborers. If they remain as laborers, they are, in fact, doomed. There are many instances in the village to show that the old bachelors simply die out after years of toiling. They have no alternative to disappearance.

To landowners, the prospect is hardly better. In Yünnan large landowners are rare; most of them possess only petty holdings. The biggest holding in the village I investigated is less than 4 acres. The average size of a farm in China is about 3.5 acres. The average holding in this village is about 5.7 mow—slightly less than 1 acre.

On a small farm there is little hope for accumulation of capital. Villagers know this well. They do not believe in the possibility of acquiring land through hard work on the land. However, as a matter of fact, there was one case of this kind. But when I mentioned it, the villagers waved aside the case contemptuously by saying that the farmer had dug a fortune in the night from his farm!

Land is closed to ambition. As the villagers put it: "Land breeds no land." Ambitious people leave the village to seek their fortunes either by holding a position in the government, by risking themselves to join the army, or by taking even more dangerous adventures in illegal traffic. If one is shocked by hearing of the unhappy choices of unrespectable ways of attaining wealth, it is up to one to create better outlets for the hard-pressed peasants. In a community where industry and commerce are not developed, where land has already done its best, and where population pressure is increasing, who is to blame when "decency" can be acquired only through crime?

Upstarts who have attained wealth come back to the village to buy land. They are the big landowners. But when they retire into the village, the pressure of population will soon wear them out—and after a few generations the big house will break down into a number of petty owners. The rise and fall of peasant families maintains the dynamic equilibrium of the traditional social structure.

The characteristic features of the traditional structure may, then, be summarized as follows: there is a surplus of labor in the village which is related to the traditional ideology of filial prosperity and the limited opportunity for employment outside of agriculture. Cheap labor gives rise to the dichotomy of the leisure class and the poor laborers. It brings a low standard of living, in general, and calls forth a nonacquisitive attitude. Under this condition technological development is blocked. But without technological improvement no expansion of natural resources is feasible, and the population pressure cannot be lifted. This is a vicious circle. It has lasted for centuries in interior China and will persist until a strong force breaks the circle.

And this leads to consideration of war conditions since 1937. We are still in the midst of struggle, and the situation is one of life or death. Despair and hope may alternately blind us to the true meaning of the present disturbance, but a hundred years from now, when the heroic episodes have faded away and when emotional tension shall have ceased to bias reflection, historians will, I think, be able to assess the less colorful, but more deeply rooted, events of this age of cultural metamorphosis that has been initiated by the long and wide struggle for national existence. It is as yet too early to say what will be the outcome of this metamorphosis, but what is already clear is the gradual breakdown of the traditional system under our eyes.

I shall try to describe a segment of the picture of the changes which have occurred in the interior villages in Yünnan.

The present war has shaken the traditional rural structure to its foundation. It calls out a vast amount of rural labor to military service and to modern industry. New opportunities are opened to the desperate peasants. Their age-long bond to the land, which has offered them nothing but a bare existence, is cut. They begin to leave the village. The outflow of rural population started in Yünnan in 1938, when I was in a village undertaking my field study, and has continued to the present time.

When I revisited my field of investigation in October, 1939—about twenty months after my first visit—there was a visible change in the village. Half of the bachelor laborers had disappeared. Most of the young men of well-to-do families had been sent away. The total number of those gone was 55 males, or 12 per cent of the total, and 19 females, or 5 per cent of the total. If we count only the adult males from sixteen to forty-five, about 27 per cent had left the village.

This was only the beginning. More must have gone since the end of 1939. If the last four years have recruited the same number of people from the village as did the first twenty months, it is likely that half of the adult male population has left the village. Among the 55 cases, I know that only 19 of them were conscripted; the rest went out to the government service, to the Yünnan-Burma Railway, which was under construction, and to newly established modern factories.

The war has taken out the population from the villages, but at the same time it has brought in wealth to the villages. The price of rural produce increased 50 per cent during the first twenty months in the years 1938–39. It has jumped rapidly to one hundred and fifty times the pre-war level by June, 1943; Kunming has risen to the top of the world price level. Inflation has promised prosperity to the rural producers.

Before 1941 the peasants paid their taxes in money. Inflation meant a reduction of their burden. Except for a few items, such as wages, the price of rice has been in the leading position of the rising tide of prices. The purchasing-power of the rice producers is steadily increasing. I think it is fair to say that the standard of living of the peasant improved during the first few years of war. It may be different since the introduction of the new principle of taxation in kind.

For the poor laborers the situation was still better. I have said that their main trouble before the war was periodical unemployment. Now they can easily get jobs and demand the highest wages. During the autumn of 1942, in the busy period of harvest, the highest wage for a male laborer in the village where I was living was one hundred dollars a day with food—30 per cent higher than the income of a professor! The average wage varied around thirty to forty or fifty dollars a day, that is, four hundred times what it was formerly. The increase in the price of rice has been, perhaps, one hundred and fifty times—which means a real increase in wages. During the first twenty months of the war, wages rose faster than the price of rice: wages rose to three times, while rice rose only to twice. The income of the laborers has been, therefore, definitely increased.

During the year 1940–41, Kunming and other large cities were constantly at the mercy of the enemy's bomber. Most of the institutions and families found shelter in the villages. They were dispersed, scattered. The newcomers to the villages are consumers. They rent houses and buy food from the villagers. They contribute to the prosperity of the rural districts. On the other hand, they bring into the villages of the interior their modernized ways of living. They are spreading modern knowledge on sanitation and modern ideas about all sorts of things.

It is unprecedented in Chinese history for a college professor or a railway construction engineer to share a house in common with a peasant. My landlady, as one result, is able to learn from my wife the way of bringing up children. And, owing to my constant interference, the beating of his wife by my landlord has become less frequent in our house than before! If the most efficient way of cultural diffusion is through direct contact and concrete demonstration, the mingling of social classes must carry weight in the cultural change in the rural community.

I have mentioned several of the outstanding features of the new situation created by the war in the rural community, namely, drainage of rural labor by military service and industry; the opening of new opportunities outside of agriculture; the increase of family income; and contact with modern culture. Now let us follow these lines to see what some of the changes are that have been called forth, and something of the problems involved.

In the autumn of 1939, the leisure class in the village found difficulty in hiring laborers. I had the opportunity to study the problem directly, and I felt the tension with the landowners. During the harvest I usually went out with them to try to hire laborers. We came back in despair. Several of them had postponed harvesting their crops in the hope that helping hands would appear. But the situation was disappointing, and finally most of the lazy landowners had to take up the farm work themselves. It was hard for them: Once I found my friend, Uncle Chang, in the field without his long gown. He was painfully embarrassed and made all possible excuses for such an undignified undertaking. He left the field at once, invited us to tea, and spent the rest of the day with us—to show that he was still a member of the leisure class. The traditional ideology evidently tortured him. But the shortage of laborers and rising wages forced him to cast off his face as well as his gown. The leisure class was threatened; in fact, for the time being it was doomed.

The leisure class represented the dormant labor force under the traditional structure. The members were mobilized when the active labor force was drained away from the village. Many had been worrying about the labor supply in the rural community during the war. They thought that the outflow of man-power from the village would affect the productivity of the land and eventually would affect the food supply at large. But, after six years of war, there is no indication of real danger.

This is owing to the fact that in the traditional structure a large part of the labor force has been kept in reserve. When the dormant labor force is mobilized, however unwillingly, it is quite sufficient to make up for the outflowing laborers. The traditional dichotomy of leisure and toil becomes less and less apparent. A new form of rural structure will emerge and will, probably, take the form of a community of occupying owners. In this form of structure the grave problem of tenancy as found in coastal and central China will not appear, unless other forces bring about a concentration of landownership.

The outflow of population from the rural area will definitely lift a part of the population pressure on the land. But, if we examine the nature of emigration, we shall see that there is a grave side to the picture. Those who leave the village belong mostly to the younger generation. They are gone forever; they will not return to the land.

The traditional attitude of despising farm labor exists as before. I have interviewed a number of young country boys who have left their homes. Even for those who are not successful in their new careers, the idea of returning to agriculture does not enter their minds. One of our Research Fellows has recorded a long discussion with a landowner who was worrying over the fact that when he is too old there will be no one to continue the work of managing his farm. The old man is right when he says that it is a pity his sons do not realize the danger of becoming men without land. There is danger of a discontinuity in farming experience. To manage a farm requires knowledge which is transmitted orally and by example from father to son. A successful farm manager always possesses minute knowledge of his farm. When the sons come back after a long period of drifting in the outside world, even with the best intention to return to the land, they may find they are not at all prepared to succeed their deceased father.

That old man said, again, that it is probable he will rent his land to tenants when he becomes unable to manage it himself. He is one of many and represents a common problem of landowners. There must, therefore, be another radical change in the rural structure.

The discontinuity of farming experience is but one part of the process of the disturbance of tradition. The ecological reshaping is significant in its social and cultural bearings. It means a reform of social structure and a readjustment of individual personality. When the younger generation acquires a set of new experiences which are so different from those of the older generation, the social unity of the old and the young is challenged. They cannot understand each other even though they are still linked by the old social ties.

Conflicts are unavoidable. The elder son of my land-lord ran away from home three times after the announcement of his betrothal, which, in accordance with immemorial custom, had been arranged by his parents. He had not returned at the time I left. He attempted to join the ground staff of the air force; then he attempted to join a new factory. But the hard life of the outside world and the insistence of his father twice made him return. But at last he went to join the army training school and stayed there. His father was perplexed and frequently came to me for consultation. He could not understand why the youngsters were so stubborn and wild. They are changed and will go on changing while they are away.

Even more difficult for the parents to deal with are their daughters. In the traditional village structure, women are farm laborers. Even in well-to-do families of the village, girls are not free from taking part in farm work. Now newly introduced factories are recruiting girls. Factory work is much lighter and more interesting than toiling in the mud. Attracted by high wages and urban life, girls rush to the city with or without the permission of their parents. They come back with bare legs, on high heels—and with permanent waves! Betrothals, previously arranged by their families, are broken, and romantic dreams bewilder their outlook.

War has thus succeeded in bringing country boys and girls to a new world. It has robbed the new generation of their tradition and of their parents. The economic reward for social values is now precisely the reverse of what it formerly was. Now, the merchant is first; then comes the factory laborer, then the peasants, and then the scholars. The world is upside down from the viewpoint of the traditional scale of social values.

And what are the prospects for present-day youth? There are opportunities, but opportunities are vain to those who have no preparation to make use of them!

Jobs are easy to find during the war, but only those who are fit can stay on. The rural-minded and mostly illiterate youngsters with vague and wild ambitions are recruited to the cities. Like the son of my landlord, they soon find that city life is attractive, but in no sense comfortable. They are not satisfied to do the low jobs, because, as someone told me, these jobs are not promising. I discovered that, in their dreams, some of these boys will not be satisfied unless they can attain a position comparable to mine! The confused standards during wartime are responsible for their bewilderment.

It is even true, however, that one may become rich in a fortnight. There are concrete instances, such as that of the car driver who married a beautiful modern girl and lived in a most expensive hotel after one trip to Burma. The outside world, as envisaged in the minds of the villagers, is usually full of gold, everywhere.

We have made several studies in modern factories in order to follow these villagers into their city life. It is rather discouraging to hear the remarks factory managers make. On the basis of several years' experience, they have begun to distrust the local laborers. The difficulty in converting rural hands directly into factory laborers is apparent. The inefficiency and lack of discipline of the local laborers become tiresome to the managers.

Moreover, the responsiveness of the recently rural laborer to the financial incentive is at times weak. Those who come from the village know well that the villagers come to the city seeking something quite beyond the ability of the factory management to offer. The village is now enjoying prosperity—so a son of a well-to-do family does not worry too much about his income. He can always ask for money from his father. And we know that many local laborers in the factory are receiving subsidies from their families. What they want are exemption from army service and a better social status. When their jobs do not answer their wants, they move on. The high rate of turnover has alarmed factory management.

In 1941 the government had to adopt a long-view policy of training modern workers from an early age. At the present time most of the national factories can depend on their own trained young workers and have stopped recruiting adults from the country.

What kind of education is now given to youth in the factory? Thousands of youngsters about twelve years of age have been recruited to the factories, where they are carefully regimented. The family tie has been cut; they will not go back. It is impossible to train a child who is always going back to the farm and keeping in touch with the life there. The managements of the factories claim they must have the child from the very beginning, in order to create a really efficient, modern, factory worker. After one or two years of training, and discipline in a military sense, they become efficient factory workers. That is the way the factory managements are educating the young army of industrialists. They are very easily regimented; urgency demands use of this method. The young laborers learn to read. They develop their way of material living. For that we must give credit to Western civilization.

The system is neither good nor bad. It was the same in Russia and Japan. We are hoping for a very quick development, and everything is being prepared for the task of industrializing China. High speed is present in Kunming and around Kunming. There is no alternative left to us. We can see no possibility of existence without heavy industry in China.

The turnover of female workers in the factories is striking. In one of the cotton mills in Kunming, the average length of employment is less than six months. Every day new girls are enlisted, and old hands are asking—or are asked—to leave. Thousands of girls, with completely emancipated personalities, have been pouring out from the factories into the city. They will not go back to their country homes but will remain in the city, either married to outsiders or enjoying a free life. These girls have driven their parents to despair.

If I exaggerate the situation, it is because of repeated occurrences of sensational tales both in the villages and in the factories. Possible exaggeration may bring forth more emphatically the problems which are involved in the sudden development of metropolitan centers and the speedy change from the rural to the urban type of personality. Confusion is to be expected. I was confused, for instance, when I found my own former maid sitting beside me in the balcony of a cinema while Chaplin's *Great Dictator* was on the screen. She was in a fur coat, and with a husband who was better dressed than I. Four years before she had been only a dirty little country girl.

An incident such as this leads to consideration of another problem which I call higher income versus better living. Owing largely to rapid inflation there is a redistribution of wealth among classes. The burden of war is solely on the shoulders of those whose income is controllable by the government. Those who are free from the burden of war are mostly the less-educated people.

I hope my audience will excuse me from the charge of "sour grapes" for raising the problem of correlation between increases of income and elevation of standards of living. I wish to inquire concerning standards of living in their relation to expenditures. My experience in wartime makes me extremely aware of the danger of expanding material power without keeping pace with a sense of values. This is true in the larger aspect of modern civilization; it is true also in the daily observation of conditions in the inland villages of China. That too rapidly increased purchasing-power, intrusted to uneducated minds, may push awry the life-pattern of common people is as true as that the power of directing a nation's destiny leads to tragedy when intrusted to a madman like Hitler. The difference is merely that the former ruins a house, while the latter ruins a world.

My landlord, despite a rapid increase in his family income, last year sold several mow of land. That was because, with money in his hand, he became much more addicted to the gambling table. If we take standards of living as a basis, or measuring-rod, for human welfare and happiness, I would hesitate to say that there has been any improvement in his house.

I must not, of course, minimize certain general improvements in the material life of the peasants during the last few years. They do have better food and better clothing, including foreign-styled overcoats for the village elders. However, much more can be done than has been done with the increase in income of the peasant.

If I am asked only to describe rural conditions in interior China during the war, I am glad to be able to give you a picture which is in no sense worse than that of the pre-war period. It is an entirely different matter if I am asked whether such a redistribution of wealth is justifiable during wartime. I, who have been with the peasants for many years and who know well how they have been misruled for centuries, feel satisfaction in observing that their living conditions are better. But I must admit that this temporary relief does not appear to me to promise a happy prospect. The rural population will increase within a short period, and a new revolution of the wheel will ensue. There is a strong belief among certain influential groups in China that man-power is more important than spiritual power in a national struggle. Traditional ideology is still deeply rooted among the peasants. How far modern industry, if developed, can prove a solution to the fundamental population problem in China is open to doubt. The discontinuance of tradition among, and social control of, the younger generation, who have to a considerable degree been spoiled by the social confusion incidental to the war, has disheartened not only their fathers but also more or less farsighted sociologists.

The problems mentioned above seem to indicate a serious lag between opportunity and capacity, between the material and the spiritual life. The solution is obvious and simple; it is to be found in one word—education. But to realize that solution means an entire reconstruction of Chinese culture from the bottom to the top. I am glad that we shall have a chance to listen to a discussion of this problem at our next meeting under the direction of our veteran Professor Chin.

ECONOMIC RECONSTRUCTION AND PLANNING: WARTIME AND POST-WAR

By WU CHING-CHAO

WHEN, in 1937, war broke out between China and Japan, the Chinese government decided as its fundamental policy to intensify the work of reconstruction in order to augment our power of resistance. This policy is all the more important because the interior of China, which we knew must become the base for the sustenance of our war effort, had been little developed industrially before 1937.

There was not, for example, a single blast furnace in the whole district which is now designated as Free China. There was not a single coal mine which had an annual production of more than 100,000 tons. Of more than 5,000,000 spindles which China possessed before the war, only 17,000 were in this area. Of the railways which China had built before the war, all were lost to the enemy except a few hundred miles of the western end of the Lung-Hai Railway and the middle section of the Hankow-Canton Railway. In a word, from the viewpoint of industrialization, what is now known as Free China was very backward.

Fortunately, in foodstuffs, Free China is self-sufficient and rich in many kinds of raw materials. Since food is the most important item of war needs, the government has tried to insure an adequate supply of the staples, particularly rice and wheat. Many methods have been used, such as dissemination of better seeds, eradication of insects and pests, and extension of irrigation works.

According to official reports, the farms of Free China yielded 48,000,000 more piculs—a picul is about 133 pounds—of foodstuffs in 1942 than in the year preceding. Recently we have often heard of the possible economic collapse of China. It may be confidently said that so long as Free China reaps a bumper crop there is no possibility of an economic collapse. Chinese history shows that many dynasties were overthrown by hungry mobs, but order was always maintained when there was no large-scale famine. That is the reason why the government adopts all means to safeguard the harvests.

In order to improve living conditions of the farmers, the government has during the last few years helped them to form co-operatives, particularly credit co-operatives. Some years ago a general survey was made relative to the rate of interest charged in the rural communities. It was found that in not a single province was the average rate of interest less than 50 per cent. That the farmers needed extension of credit at a cheaper rate was abundantly evident.

Accordingly, the government set up a Co-operative Administration, and government banks have been ordered to co-operate with this administration and to lend money to the co-operatives. At present a duly registered and recognized co-operative may borrow money from the bank at an annual rate of 9 per cent, and the farmers may borrow from the co-operative at 12 per cent. There are now nearly 30,000 co-operative societies in Free

China. In 1942 the total farm loans extended by the Farmers Bank alone—the Farmers Bank is one of the four government banks—were given at $682,000,000 Chinese. This year the Farmers Bank planned to lend $800,000,000 to the co-operatives, exclusive of $180,-000,000 for land finance.

The matter of land finance brings me to the problem of tenancy. According to statistics for 1937, 46 per cent of the farmers were owners of their land; 24 per cent were part-owners; and 30 per cent were tenants. To help part-owners and tenants to own their land, the Farmers Bank chose Peipei, Szechuan, and Wangwei-chu Irrigation District, Kansu, as experimental centers for a little pioneer work. If the results prove satisfactory, the experiment will be extended to other parts of the country.

Many persons, in China and abroad, seem to hold the idea that, if the tenancy problem in China is solved, everything will be all right with the farmers. Personally, I do not take too much stock in this idea. It seems to me that the crucial problem of our farmers is not that a part of them do not own their farms but that the average farm is too small to sustain a decent standard of living. The average size of farms in China as a whole is 22 mow, which equals only $3\frac{1}{2}$ acres.

With such a small farm it is of little importance whether one owns it or rents it—one can hardly make both ends meet in any case. It is imperative that means be devised to enlarge the average farm. This can be accomplished only if jobs, other than farming, can be found for a part of the rural population.

Industrialization will be one of the means; development of public works will be another. When these steps have been taken, many farmers will sell their small pieces of land and earn their living in other occupations. Those who remain in the country may enlarge their farms by buying the land of those who migrate to the cities. Therefore, to solve the problems of the farmers alone, industrialization is necessary.

As previously mentioned, there were but a few factories in the interior prior to 1937. As soon as the latest [the fifth] Sino-Japanese war began, the government realized that the struggle would be of long duration and that measures should be taken to develop the interior so that the fighting power of the Chinese army might not be greatly weakened by temporary loss of the coastal districts.

One of the measures adopted was to remove as many factories as possible from the coastal districts to the far interior. Among the five hundred or more factories which have been moved inland may be mentioned iron-works, machine shops, electrical supplies plants, chemical works, spinning and flour mills. In addition, new factories have been established from time to time. In the cases of iron and steel, cement, coal, oil, alcohol distilling, electrical appliances, and spinning and weaving the new capacity for production is particularly noticeable.

Before this war not a drop of gasoline had been produced; but in 1942 we produced 1,800,000 gallons, and it was planned to produce three times that amount in 1943. Because of the importance of oil for war purposes, the government has encouraged establishment of factories to produce substitutes. Among such may be mentioned alcohol. We produced 8,000,000 gallons last year, and we plan to produce 10,000,000 gallons this year [1943].

Coal production in Szechuan never passed $1\frac{1}{2}$ million tons before the war; now its production is more than 3 million tons. Our iron production in Free China before the war was insignificant; last year we produced 100,000 tons, and in 1943 we aim to produce 130,000 tons.

I have stated that before the war we had only 17,000 spindles in the interior. At present we have ten times as many; indeed, more than 170,000 spindles have been installed, and more will be put to work in the near future. Before the war there was only one paper mill employing modern machines. Its yearly production was 200 tons. Last year machine-made paper amounted to 4,250 tons, an increase of more than twenty times.

The work of industrialization is now in the hands of both government and private enterprise. Under the direction of the Ministry of Economic Affairs, the National Resources Commission now operates more than one hundred units of productive enterprises in the fields of mining, public utilities, and heavy industry. The Ministry of Economic Affairs has another subsidiary organization, the Industrial and Mining Administration, the function of which is to help private enterprise solve its problems. It extends credit to private factories and mines at low interest.

The Industrial and Mining Administration also serves as an intermediary between government banks and private enterprises. When it is convinced that a certain enterprise needs financial help and if it is not in a position to make the loan itself, the administration brings the case to the notice of the government banks and tries to secure loans for it.

It also maintains purchasing agents in the United States, Great Britain, and India. With the amount of foreign exchange granted by the government, the Industrial and Mining Administration purchases certain raw materials, also machine tools and machine parts, and stores them in different industrial centers. When private factories need these materials and tools for production, they may secure them from the administration. In extending loans and lending materials to private factories the administration is able to exert influence on the policy of production of the private section of industry.

As we look back on the accomplishment of the last few years, we can see that, although progress has been made, it has not measured up to the standard that we have set for ourselves. There are many difficulties which are not easily overcome.

First of all, we still lack a solid base of heavy industry to provide us with the tools of production that we need. There are many kinds of machinery which we ourselves are still unable to manufacture, and, with our main lines of communication with the outside world cut off by the Japanese blockade, we cannot even import what we want from other countries. In order, for example, to increase the production of our factories we must supply them with sufficient electricity. But, as yet, we are unable to manufacture big generators. For lack of an adequate supply of electricity, the existing factories in Chungking are doomed to operate at partial capacity only.

Transportation presents another difficulty. For lack of rails, we have built during the war only two railways, one from Hengyang to Kweichow, the other from Kunming to Hsufu. Both of these have been built with rails salvaged from other railways and are at present only partly completed. For lack of modern means of transportation, we have to rely mainly upon junks, carts, beasts of burden, and human carriers for movement of goods and passengers.

One specific incident last year impressed me profoundly with the importance of modern means of transportation for large-scale production. I visited one iron mill twice. The first time I went, the blast furnace, which was capable of producing 100 tons of pigiron per day, was operating at full capacity. A few months later, when I visited the mill the second time, the blast furnace had ceased completely to produce pigiron. Upon inquiry, I found that this mill depended upon a mine about 100 miles distant for its supply of iron ore. Between the mine and the location of the blast furnace there is a small river, and the iron ore had to be transported by sailboat. In winter, when the water is shallow, no boat can negotiate the stream. When the supply of ore which had taken months to accumulate had been used, the blast furnace was forced to cease operation. I cannot see how that blast furnace can be operated efficiently unless a railway is built to carry ore continuously to feed the furnace.

All these, and other, difficulties make us realize that large-scale industrialization is possible after the war only when the initial difficulty of getting started shall have been overcome by generous help from friendly nations. In the meantime, economic planning goes on apace.

From the very beginning of the war the government has been profoundly interested in this subject in a variety of phases. The generalissimo, for example, in one of his most important public addresses, early discussed the importance of co-ordinated public administration. According to his idea, there are three phases of public administration: planning, execution, and examination. These three phases must be dovetailed.

In accordance with this theory, a Central Planning Board and a Board of Examination were formed under the Supreme National Defense Council. In every ministry and every independent commission there was established at the same time a Committee of Planning and Examination. If a ministry had subsidiary organizations, they were ordered to form a committee for the same purpose.

In the spring or summer of every year, the Supreme National Defense Council issues an order mapping, in general terms, the kind of work that is to be done in the following year. When a ministry receives this order, it passes it on to its subsidiary organizations, adding detailed instructions. The subsidiary organizations, on the basis of those instructions, draw up plans stating what they hope to do the next year and the amount of work which they promise to accomplish in each quarter.

The plans of a subsidiary organization first go to the proper ministry. They are examined and co-ordinated into a single plan of that ministry by the Committee of Planning and Examination. The plan is then submitted to the Central Planning Board. When the plans of different ministries and independent commissions have arrived at the Central Planning Board, it is expected that the board will examine them and co-ordinate them into a single plan for the government as a whole.

In 1942, owing to the shortage of technical personnel in the board, it did not fully carry out this method. What it did was to grade the plans of each ministry into three classes: A, B, and C, so that when money was insufficient to put all the plans into execution, plans of the C class were dropped. In 1943 the board intended to study the plans more thoroughly and make constructive contributions.

At the end of each quarter the several organizations must prepare a report of their work. The preparing of a report follows much the same procedure. It starts from the bottom; finally all the reports reach the Board of Examination. There the reports are closely scrutinized and compared with the original plans.

Several times a year the Board of Examination sends out representatives to different parts of the country to check on the verity of the figures in the reports. On the basis of the reports and the board's own findings, a statement to the public is issued in May describing the most important work accomplished by the government in the previous year.

Besides this regular procedure, the plans and reports of every branch of the Executive Yüan are periodically examined by the plenary session of the Central Executive Committee of the Kuomintang and by the People's Political Council. Both of these organizations meet once or twice every year. In these meetings, every minister must make an oral report—which usually lasts about two hours—on what his ministry has done since the last session and what it plans to do in the future. A more lengthy written report is also submitted for examination.

The plenary session of the Central Executive Committee of the Kuomintang usually passes a resolution on the reports of the Executive Yüan as a whole, but the People's Political Council takes its work more seriously and has one resolution for each report submitted. In the resolution it points out the merits and defects of the work of each ministry and suggests ways and means of improvement. In this way the influence of public opinion is brought to bear on the work of the government.

Besides this year-by-year plan, each ministry has been asked to prepare a ten-year plan for the post-war period. In preparing the post-war long-range plan, more persons have been consulted and more works of research have been carried out. Some of the plans are now in shape; others are still in the making.

Let us take the iron and steel plan for illustration. This plan is divided into six parts. The first part reviews the iron and steel industry throughout the world, paying particular attention to such countries as the United States, Germany, Soviet Russia, Great Britain, France, and Japan. It also studies China's imports of iron and steel goods during the five-year period between 1932 and 1937 and forecasts the probable amount of iron and steel which China will need after the war in such industries as shipbuilding, railway building, mining, the machinery industry, and so on.

The second part deals with the location of future iron and steel industries in China. More than ten locations have been selected for examination. Each location is studied with reference to the supply of raw materials and the kind of demand that will probably arise from the near-by districts.

The third part deals with the products which each iron and steel mill is supposed to manufacture.

The fourth part deals with the nature and quality of iron ores and coking coal in different parts of China.

The fifth part deals with refractory materials, and the last part deals with the number of staff members and skilled laborers required in all the iron and steel mills. A table is then attached to the original plan, showing the amount of capital required to realize this plan.

In drawing up a plan such as that for iron and steel, not only have the technical members of the Ministry of Economic Affairs been mobilized, but in every step of preparation responsible persons of the Ministry of Communication, the Office of Ordnance of the Ministry of War, and other related organizations have been invited to attend and to express their opinions.

The main reason for such a conference is that the supply of iron and steel must be co-ordinated with the demand which will come partly from other fields outside the jurisdiction of the Ministry of Economic Affairs. When this plan is submitted to the Central Planning Board, it will be further studied and discussed by a committee of experts from different governmental, financial, and industrial organizations.

More than twenty-five years ago Dr. Sun Yat-sen wrote a book which became famous, *The International Development of China*. This work was published shortly after the first World War. At that time Dr. Sun noted that there were surplus plants and equipment in many Western countries; he hoped that, instead of being scrapped, some might be transplanted to China to develop our people's natural resources. Unfortunately, his proposal fell on deaf ears at home and abroad. Now, again, we have come to a situation similar to that which incited Dr. Sun to write his book.

Guided by the teachings of Dr. Sun and encouraged by the declaration of the Atlantic Charter, particularly the provision of Article VII of the Mutual Aid Agreements and the statement of Secretary Hull in July, 1942, to the effect that machinery should be devised through which capital may, for the development of the world's resources and for the stabilization of economic activity, move on equitable terms from financially stronger to financially weaker countries, we have made our plans with the anticipation that our allies will help us in our gigantic work of economic development.

"But," one may ask, "in what ways can foreign countries co-operate with China in its economic development?" First of all, I think the easiest and the least expensive way is to lend us some of the $15,000,000,000 worth of wartime industrial plants which the government of the United States has built and owns. There are, roughly speaking, about 1,500 such plants, including 395 aircraft factories, 70 arms plants, 54 radio and communications equipment plants, 161 machine-tool factories, 42 shipyards and plants making ship parts, 57 iron and steel projects, 43 aluminum plants, 24 magnesium plants, 22 plants producing other metals, and 10 synthetic rubber factories and plants making ingredients of synthetic rubber.

For many of these plants, after the war, the United States will have no use. In fact, if all of them are allowed to operate at full capacity, they will soon create a glut in the domestic market. In view of this, some of these plants must be disposed of in one way or another. And, may I ask, is it not best to lend some of them to a country like China, which needs them urgently?

All these plants have been paid for from the current expenditures of the government. Therefore the United States government would not, by lending some of these plants to China on a long-term contract, add a cent of burden to American taxpayers. When China repays its debt, the proceeds may help the United States government to retire its huge public debt. In this way the United States can help itself by helping China.

Another method by which our friends may co-operate with us is for private industrialists to make direct investments in China. We have natural resources and labor power, but we do not possess sufficient capital goods. If American industrialists should ship some capital goods to China, production along many lines can be started immediately, thereby creating profit for themselves and money income for our people.

In 1940 there were approximately two thousand American corporations that had direct investments to the amount of $7,000,000,000 in foreign countries. When I learned that China has received only $46,000,000, or less than 1 per cent of this huge sum, I had the feeling that our market had been grossly neglected. I hope that after the war we shall be more favorably considered.

Some people hold to the erroneous notion that an industrial China will be a strong competitor of the United States in the world market and that, therefore, it is to the interest of the United States to keep China permanently in an agricultural economy. They forget that increased production in other countries will not reduce, but rather will raise, living standards in the United States. For a prosperous United States many prosperous neighbors, to absorb the products of its factories and farms, are needed.

It is not by chance that the most industrialized countries of the world are at the same time the best customers of this country. They have more purchasing-power and are consequently able to consume more American goods. In 1936, one year before the outbreak of the latest Sino-Japanese war, American exports to the United Kingdom amounted to $440,000,000, while those to China came to only one-tenth of that sum. Had China been as industrialized as the United Kingdom and possessed the same purchasing-power per capita, then China, with a population ten times as great as the United Kingdom, should have bought from this country not merely $46,000,000 of American goods but more than $4,000,000,000 worth!

If we could achieve that goal, what a boom it would create in the American market! It seems to me that in discussing international economic co-operation in the future, we must look upon our neighbors more as customers and less as competitors.

In this connection I should also like to make an observation that there are two kinds of industrialized nations. One kind is represented by the United States and Soviet Russia; the other is represented by Japan and Germany. The first type of country possesses rich natural resources and a big market at home; the second type is not so well endowed and must rely heavily on other countries, both as a source of foodstuffs and raw materials and as a market for manufactured goods.

China, if industrialized, will belong to the first category. We have the largest domestic market: our demand for goods can never be adequately satisfied. When we develop an iron and steel industry, we shall supply rails for our own railroads and steel parts for our own ships. When we develop a machine industry, we shall supply tools of production for our own factories.

The whole program of industrialization in China is oriented toward meeting the needs and demands of a huge domestic market. We are more interested in raising our own living standards than in snatching markets from others. This does not mean that we shall not pay attention to our exports. On the contrary, we want to increase our exports as best we can in order in part to finance our imports. But our exports will comprise those goods which we can produce to advantage and for which we have already established a market in the world. We shall continue to export such articles as silk, tea, tung oil, soybeans, bristles, embroideries, tungsten, antimony, tin, and so on, in exchange for capital goods which we need for large-scale industrialization.

While I wish to emphasize the importance of American help in the economic development of China as an undertaking beneficial to both parties, I must not leave the impression that China will be hopeless if that help is not forthcoming. There are capital markets in other parts of the world. If we should fail to get what we want from the United States, we shall look elsewhere for what we need, and if the worse comes to the worst, and no one will help us, may God help those who help themselves!

If necessary, we may try to control the channels of international trade and resort to such devices as high tariffs, barter, the quota system, and exchange control in order to get as much foreign exchange as possible into the hands of the government so that we may import the necessary instruments of production to build up our industry. That would bring hardships and sufferings to our own people, and its repercussions would be damaging to world economy and world peace. I sincerely hope that we shall not be compelled to do this because of lack of international co-operation.

EDUCATION IN CONTEMPORARY CHINA

By CHIN YUEH-LIN

I FIND myself in a very embarrassing predicament. I am a sort of jack of some trades and master of none. My colleagues in this conference are experts, and I am not an expert in any line. My field has been logic and epistemology for a number of years, and I think I may as well say that in that field there is no expert. If there were experts, they probably wouldn't be philosophers.

It happens that this is a rather peculiar subject, and so I feel diffident when I come before you to try to talk about education. From the bottom of my heart I crave your indulgence.

Now, speaking very frankly, I don't know exactly what education is. Mathematical logic—a subject in which I have been interested for some time—is defined by Mr. Bertrand Russell as a subject in which we do not know what we are talking about—or whether what we say is true. I don't know definitely, clearly, in terms of distinct and clear ideas, what education is. I take it for granted that it is the kind of thing that schools and universities are engaged in, and I shall take it up in that sense only.

I have some statistics here which may not be adequately interpreted, since I do not understand them thoroughly. We may divide education into the customary primary, secondary, and higher education. I shall start with quantity. Experts on education may laugh at that term. I couldn't think of any other, so I speak in terms of quantity.

Possibly one of the things that will surprise you is the increase in the numbers of students in China. During your war years, your colleges and schools are somewhat depleted, whereas in China there is actually an increase in the number of students in both middle (i.e., high) schools and universities. I do not know whether that is true of students in the primary schools, but I believe it is. The figures here are not comparative as far as primary education is concerned.

From 1936 to 1937 the number of universities and colleges was 36; from 1937 to 1938, 29; from 1938 to 1939, 32; from 1939 to 1940, 36; from 1940 to 1941, 41; and from 1941 to 1942, 45. There is, then, an increase in the number of higher institutions. These figures are for the government universities. There is a decrease in what are known as private universities. We started with 42 in 1936 and we had only 38 in 1941.

The number of students in colleges, universities, and technical schools in 1936 was 41,922. In 1941 there were 59,000 students—that is, roughly, the number of university students has increased in five years from 41,000 to 59,000. That is a rather big increase in university and college students. I am using the word "university" to cover colleges and technical schools.

For the middle school, there is the same kind of increase. In 1936–37 we had 627,000 students; in 1940–41, 768,000.

The number of students in primary schools in 1941–42 was around 22,000,000. This last figure is not comparative. We have no previous figures, so we don't know whether there is an increase or not, but at the time my colleagues and I left Chungking in the latter part of May [1943], the minister of education told us there was quite an increase in the number of primary students also.

So, in primary, secondary, and higher education we have an increase in the number of students.

Now, as to quality: by "quality" I might mean a number of things, but I am speaking of standards. Put it this way: Before the war there were certain standards of excellence. As compared with that, the standard has been very much lowered—and, it is believed, the trend is toward a still greater lowering, so that there is a distinct deterioration of quality.

We may start with the primary school. Previous to the war [1937], primary schools were manned by administrators and teachers, many of whom have now gone into other lines of work. Of those that remain, the quality of teachers is probably not comparable to the quality of the teachers before the war. I do not know personally the conditions of primary schools. Not having children, I suppose I yield to a certain laziness, but I have never bothered about the primary schools with which my friends are concerned.

Take the school in the village where I lived with a friend. I heard my friend complaining all the time about it. I think, even in terms of health education, that that school lags very much behind some of the other schools to which my friends are accustomed. This friend of mine has two children of school age in my village. Both of them attend school; after a few weeks both had two lines of bluish liquid running from their nostrils all the time—a condition which did not exist before they entered the school. Moreover, they are eternally catching cold. Aside from this kind of thing that I occasionally hear my friends speak of, I have no firsthand knowledge.

Neither do I have such knowledge of the secondary schools. I think that previous to the war we had very few good secondary schools. I believe my colleagues will bear out that statement. As far as my experience is concerned with entrance examinations and things of that nature, the middle school in Peking attached to the Normal University, the Nankai Middle School in Tientsin, and the Yangchow Middle School were all very good middle schools, at least good preparatory schools for university education.

I don't know where they are now. Somebody in the audience may be able to tell me whether the Yangchow School is still in existence and, if so, where it is. Nankai is still in Chungking. But in the middle schools we have a question that I shall take up a bit later on in connection with higher education.

In the middle schools we also have the problem of teachers. The teachers there are generally young men with a good deal of ambition and possibly with less attachment to their schools and their profession than is the case with some of the university professors. At the same time their salaries are very low, and it is perfectly possible for a teacher in the middle school to be talking about the standard of living and the cost of living instead of mathematics or physics or whatever the subject may be.

Then there is a question of the teachers' leaving. A lot of them enter government service or the factories run by the National Resources Commission or the Ordnance Department or other factories or railroads or other branches of government service. Hence it has been difficult to retain middle-school teachers, except during the last year or so. I think there has been some difference in the last year, but previous to that time it was extremely difficult to retain teachers. From this alone one can easily see there would be a decrease in the quality of secondary education.

Concerning higher education, I have more direct experience. There are a number of things which contribute toward its deterioration. On the whole, I should say that if we continue the war for, let us say, five years, we shall probably need five years for recovery; that is to say, a total of ten years is needed to return to pre-war standards. If we continue over ten years, we shall probably need somewhere around another ten years for recovery.

With the pre-war standard as the starting-point, the war seems to me to have retarded educational progress for a period that is double the period of the war.

One reason which is peculiar to some universities, and not to others, is the lack of books and equipment. Some universities are not so much affected, although they are affected from the point of view of new books. Some universities have moved from their original location to a distant location with their books and some of their equipment. Of course, they are bound to lose certain things. It has been difficult to remove engineering equipment when that consisted of large and heavy machinery. With regard to books, some universities were fortunate in being able to remove a large number to the interior; but other universities, such as Tsinghua University, Peking University, and Nankai University, were not so fortunate. Peking was lost on July 29, 1937, before most of the things could be moved. In fact, we members of the faculty had to sneak out. Most of the things were left in Peking.

Nankai, in particular, has been a sort of battle-ground, so that the damage to Nankai University is probably much more thorough than to other universities.

There is, for these universities, almost a 90 per cent loss of property—95 per cent probably, and, I think, in some cases you might as well say 100 per cent, loss of property in terms of equipment and books. Even for those who are more fortunate the problem of new books and things is as difficult as for any other university.

In Lien Ta, which is the Southwest Associated University, that is to say, the combination of National Peking University, National Tsinghua University, and Nankai University, there are few books at the present time, and there is generally a fight for those books—a run for them. It is pathetic to see students hurrying through their dinner in the evening to stick around the door of the library trying to get ahead of one another, and stationing themselves as near to the door as possible so that, when the door opens, they may rush to the desk to get hold of their books.

Not being a scientist, I am unable to discuss the matter of equipment; but one can easily see that, for those universities which have lost their equipment, there is no way to replace it, so that there is a general lack of equipment. As a consequence, there is little experimentation going on so far as this particular university, Lien Ta, is concerned. I think in some other universities the conditions are more favorable. This is one element in the deterioration of quality of higher education.

There is another element which is something like this. Previous to the war, Tsinghua University held every year competitive examinations in various parts of China—for instance, in Peking, in Shanghai, in Canton, and in Hankow—in which generally more than three thousand students participated. I believe a little over three hundred were admitted as Freshmen, so that one out of ten, roughly, is admitted to the university. There is, therefore, a choice of the brighter students among the applicants.

Probably the same proportion holds concerning Pei Ta, that is, Peking National University. I do not know of other universities, but after the war was started we did not have that ratio, and the reason is to some extent plain. There were a number of young men who were left behind in the occupied territory. At first, perhaps, they were not of university age. Suppose a person was somewhere around fourteen or fifteen when the war started. After a few years that person becomes of university age. It would be desirable for him to attend the university. Well, he wants to go to a university in Free China, in the unoccupied territory.

Now suppose he takes a very strict entrance examination. Some of these people would not be admitted; they would not be able to get themselves admitted.

They will be stranded somewhere, and they will be very much discouraged. It is, accordingly, advisable from a number of points of view—certainly political as well as other points of view—to lower the standards of admittance so that a larger number of young men from occupied territory may study in Free China.

At first communications were rather easy. Students could take boats from Shanghai, or from Peking, or pass by Hongkong, and get to the hinterland. Later the trip wasn't so easy, and latterly we have heard touching tales of young men coming to the universities in Free China. Two of them whom I know traveled all the way on foot from Peking to Chengtu and, finally, I believe, took trucks to Kunming. They traveled from the northeast corner of China to the uttermost southwest. They had to walk practically all the way from Peking to Loyang. These two certainly walked all that way; after that, they walked quite a bit but probably caught a bus or a truck or a train part of the way.

You will agree that such men have to be taken care of in some way. One method of taking care of them is to give them what they want. If they want to study in the university, the university takes them; and, while they were not well prepared in the occupied territory (and after they come to the university they are not likely to be well trained either), on account of the lack of equipment and books and things, they do enter a university in Free China.

In some places—this is not true everywhere—there is the question of air raids and there is the question of the attractions of other kinds of life that might be taken up simultaneously with university education. These elements all tend toward a deterioration of quality, so that, on the whole, I should say, although there is an increase in quantity, there is a deterioration in quality of education.

Quantity is definitely increasing. To what extent—how much—it has increased, I really do not know, although I have read you the statistics. I am inclined to say that these statistics are more or less exact—or more or less inexact! I don't know which to say. I suppose it depends upon your attitude. Anyway, the trend of those figures indicates definitely an increase in quantity.

Of the deterioration in quality I am more convinced. That is to say, I feel definitely that there *is* a deterioration.

I now take up a point that has nothing to do with quantity or quality. Well, it may have something to do with quality—that is, direction and purpose. I shall not take up quantity and quality again, except as they come out in the discussion. But as far as direction and purpose are concerned, I should say a few words.

I take it for granted that the purpose of education—the kind of thing that schools and universities are meant for—is to produce a certain development in character, a certain rounding-out of individual character development. There are some intrinsic purposes. I, personally, have been interested more in the intrinsic purpose of education.

For instance, I believe someone suggested last evening that an educated person is one who keeps custody of what has been obtained before and then plunges ahead to improve upon it in the future. Well, education has that purpose—has that more or less intrinsic purpose—

from the point of view of human civilization. I do not know whether any of you have thought of this supposition: suppose human beings stopped education for fifty years. I mean stopped completely. I don't mean going on with it surreptitiously, but stopped completely—stopped learning, stopped learning how to write, stopped learning how to read books. If you want to do a thorough job, suppose all the books were burned. I am not in favor of it, in actuality, you understand! But suppose that were the case. I said fifty years because I am Chinese, but perhaps we had better make it a hundred years, because I am conscious that English and Americans now live to ninety or a hundred years rather easily. I don't think we Chinese do very often.

Suppose you figure it at one hundred years that education is completely stopped. Then I think we would return to what somebody would call the bliss of Adam and Eve days. We wouldn't be able to know anything about history. The children born after that one hundred years of absence of education wouldn't be able to know anything of history, wouldn't be able to know anything of science, anything of the accumulated knowledge that has been passed on to us from our forefathers.

Presumably they would be able to start inquiries of their own; but, presumably, if education stopped completely for one hundred years, it would take three or four thousand years for mankind to develop again to the present stage of human knowledge. From that point of view, one can see that education has its intrinsic value from the point of view of knowledge. And, then, from the point of view of human character building, of understanding of human beings, of behaving in society, of spiritual or moral development, education has its own intrinsic values.

But, aside from that, there is another value that we can't very well ignore: that is education to answer certain national purposes. I don't think we can dismiss this element. After all, education has to serve some national purpose. Maybe, to some of us, this is not of value; but, to a number of us—especially to those of us in China—you can easily see that it is of value. That is to say, education has to serve national purposes aside from intrinsic purposes, and it is that element of which I want to speak next.

National defense involves industrialization and mechanization. I can sympathize with most of my countrymen and with the government in wanting speedy industrialization and speedy mechanization of the country. The government feels keenly the responsibility that rests with it of putting China on such a basis that it can be comparatively secure from invasion.

When war finally came in 1937, some of us in Peiping were definitely relieved in certain ways. I want to convey to you how we felt and why. Previous to 1937, from 1931 onward—indeed, throughout that long period—the people in Peiping all had the feeling: What is Japan going to do next? What will Japan do tomorrow? There was always apprehension, always that tension, which is extremely annoying, extremely uncomfortable. It made life tense, so that when war finally came it was a relief. We got the feeling that at last we were going to have a showdown. The government people, too, felt that way, naturally. It was perfectly plain that China could not remain as it was. China must be industrialized and mechanized to some extent, in order to secure a certain minimum of security against invasion at just any moment.

I sympathize with the government and my people for desiring security, that kind of security which can be obtained only by mechanization, by industrialization, and by modernization. Essentially, after all, it is a question of modernization.

Now education must help along that line. The old education certainly does not work in the twentieth century. I don't think any of my colleagues have gone through the very old style of education. I had a period of it—the classical education. I was taught to recite the four books, the *Book of Rites*, the *Book of Changes*, the *Book of Odes*, and so on. I had to recite those things without understanding them at all. I was taught to read them, and then to recite them. At the end of the year, I had to take the examination on about ten volumes, standing about a foot high on the table on the teacher's desk. I had to turn my back and start from the first line in a book and just go on reciting to the very last sentence of that book—that kind of thing. I know I was rather naughty when I recited the *Book of Changes*. I did something dishonest and was thoroughly punished for it. Otherwise, I think I passed through without a hitch!

But that kind of education—which has been going on for ages—certainly won't make China modern. The kind of education that came as a substitute for that old form of education, which was officially abolished in 1905, isn't particularly suited, either. We have universities that are divided into departments: for example, the philosophy department or the history department, more or less according to the American plan. And it seems that, from the point of view of quick industrialization and modernization, there is a demand for students who go to engineering schools and, possibly, study economics, but chiefly study engineering and subjects allied to engineering.

I understand there is an idea of producing two million engineers within the next ten years—or, I don't know how many years. To do that we have to modify the present system of education to answer the purposes of national defense, industrialization, and mechanization.

The result is at the present time quite noticeable, even in universities, and, I think, in secondary schools, too. That is to say, there is a flocking of students into engineering and some of them into economics. There is comparatively little interest in pure science and very little interest in the arts.

Now it is not merely the arts—not merely literature and philosophy and history—that are affected, but also pure science, such as chemistry and physics. We used to have a very strong department of physics at Tsinghua University near Peking; it generally had the best students admitted to the university. At the present time it is difficult to attract students to the study of physics. I think this is to some extent true also of chemistry and of the other pure sciences.

The tendency for China to go into intensely practical studies in order to bring about a speedy industrialization and mechanization is already here. The tendency is both planned and caused by circumstances. Even if there were no policy to encourage this tendency, the tendency would probably have come about anyhow. The present generation of young men probably feels that there is much more future in engineering and economics than in anything else. If a young man has a personal equation as well as the national interest at heart, he is likely to go into one of those branches.

I say the tendency is probably natural, and even without encouragement young men, from the point of view either of their own personal interest or of national interest, will probably flock to those branches instead of going to other branches. But at the same time there is a policy that encourages the taking-up of engineering and economics.

I have said that I sympathize with the government in its desire to have quick mechanization and industrialization for national defense. I think I myself believe in that, to some extent, and I can see that, if there is no other alternative, we simply have to industrialize and try to mechanize in a great hurry. I don't want to leave the impression that I am opposed to industrialization. I think it is inevitable, and in order to be able to exist as a nation we simply have to industrialize.

But what I do not like to see is the haste in which we are trying to do it. If we want to speed the process within a period of, let's say, ten or twenty or thirty years, I can see consequences which would make me extremely uncomfortable, to say the least, and which, I think, will probably have a rather bad effect not alone in China but elsewhere.

I shall speak of some of those consequences later. I shall at the present time think in terms of the policy of encouraging the kind of education that is intended to speed up industrialization in a great hurry.

I myself think that we shall not succeed in industrializing ourselves sufficiently to give us the kind of security that we intend to have through the speeding-up of industrialization. I find myself at a loss to express myself adequately. I have this kind of idea in mind: in order to industrialize, we need not only engineers, not only economists. We need, as well, pure scientists and, I think, the arts also, as well as the pure sciences. That is to say, I feel that the whole attempt toward industrialization is a synthetic one.

In order to industrialize or mechanize, what is needed is not merely engineering and all that "practical stuff," but something else as well. I think it is easy to establish that we need pure science, that if we lack pure science we shall not have very good engineering. Physics and chemistry are as much needed for industrialization as for anything else.

Let us take the example of the present war. We trained a bit of an air force before the war started. We got quite a number of planes, some of them from Italy, I think. There were also planes from America. They went in to fight at the beginning of the war. The training of aviators has been continued. During the five years that I stayed in Kunming, I saw a good deal of the air cadets there, and I am familiar with the names of a number of planes—the Hawk, the Douglas E-15 and E-16 (which they call "Buffaloes"), and a large variety of others—but most of them are such that one doesn't hear of them any more. They weren't adequate, with the change of machines of the enemy. At first the Chinese air force could go up and fight a bit, but gradually it couldn't.

Of the air cadets I knew personally, all of them were killed except two. One of them is now somewhat of an invalid; the other is still going on. I think he has the best luck in the world!

One thing, of course, is that we do not manufacture airplanes. We depend upon airplanes from abroad. The question is: Can we manufacture airplanes? We might try it. But if we want to manufacture airplanes which are up to date and capable of dealing with airplanes manufactured in other countries, in enemy countries, we must have aeronautical engineering, and you can easily see that that involves physics, chemistry—and a number of other things—and if we do not have good aeronautical engineers we shan't be able to manufacture airplanes of our own.

So you see that, even in that one single line, the question of building an air force or an airplane industry, we require pure scientists. We must encourage pure science as well. We can easily see that other things are closely related. Consequently, I am inclined to think that if we want to industrialize quickly—or at all—it is not merely engineering that needs to be studied, but also an enormous number of other subjects. And if we emphasize engineering too much, or alone, we shall not succeed in mechanizing and industrializing.

The attempt to speed up engineering education for the purpose of national security will not succeed. By attempting this thing in a great hurry, by suiting education to that speedy industrialization and mechanization, we shan't get the kind of security that industrialization or mechanization is supposed to give us.

The policy of encouraging engineering and economics at the expense of other subjects would not be adequate to give us a quick industrialization and mechanization so as to give us, in turn, the kind of security that we need. I, personally, am inclined to think that as far as education is concerned we have to attempt it more slowly.

This is speaking from the point of view of adequacy— and I think this thing is not adequate. But there is another point of view, and that is whether it is desirable. If we overemphasize certain elements in education, certain branches of knowledge, it is not desirable. If we return to some of the intrinsic purposes of education— for instance, the preservation of knowledge and the encouragement of knowledge, and the building-up of human character—if, I say, we return to some of these intrinsic values of education, we can easily see that too much emphasis, or too much diversion of young men into one or two even admittedly very useful lines, will not give us the kind of citizens that some of us want.

On the whole, I believe that the new tendency in education is inadequate for the purposes for which it is intended. From another point of view, moreover, I consider it undesirable.

In the attempt to bring about industrialization and modernization and to obtain results speedily, I am afraid the whole population will gradually become regimented: regimented in such a way that education may become mere training, and human beings, with free individual characteristics, may be turned into atoms in the social structure—and not free atoms, either. The entire social organization of China may be whipped into something like an organism with very little individual initiative. I don't like to say this, but I can't help it. I think, in the process of attaining very quick industrialization, there is the danger that we may become totalitarian in structure, and that is something which I am afraid of—and it is something which I think Americans should be afraid of, too.

From my point of view, in order that we may prevent that, it seems to me we must have a world plan, a postwar world plan. I don't know what that plan should be—in fact, I have no definite ideas on the subject—but I think we must have a world plan after the war so that security may be given to individual nations from the point of view of the world as a whole; not from the point of view only of an individual nation trying to attain its own security.

I have that subject at heart more than any other subject. I speak of education merely as a road, as a channel, to lead up to that subject.

It has been said, "Some people are born great, some people achieve greatness, and some people have greatness thrust upon them." With regard to nations we have a similar case. I do not know whether America was born a great leader or whether America achieved leadership. In any case, leadership is thrust upon America; and it seems to me that in America we have to think in terms of world plans in order to avoid future wars, and in order to avoid regimentation here and elsewhere as a weapon for security.

I am sure I am not making myself clear. My English gets extremely rusty so that I don't express myself clearly, but I have wanted to present that problem as a problem for the consideration of all present. I thank you for the opportunity to voice a part of my ideas on the subject.

INDEX

Academia Sinica, xxxix

Advancement of China, 10–15

Aeronautical engineering, 96

Agriculture: mechanization of, xlii–xliii; and problem of nutrition, 22

All China Congress, 4, 13

American Bureau for Medical Aid to China, 43

Animal husbandry, and problem of nutrition, 22–23

Army, naturalization of, 11

Army Medical College, 42

Army Medical Service, 27, 40

Army training schools, xlvi; curriculum of, xlvii

Atlantic Charter, 76

Beriberi, 19

Birth control, xxiv, xxxii–xxxiv, xliii, 32–33

Birth rate, high, xxiv

Bisson, T. A., xxvi; xix n.

Bland, J. O. P., xxxi–xxxii

Board of Examination, 72, 73

Borsodi, Ralph, "Must China Endure This Too?" xxvii–xxviii

Central Control Committee, 4, 5, 6

Central Executive Committee, xvii, xviii, 2, 4, 73–74; Standing Committee of, 5, 6

Central Field Health Station, 26–27, 38–39

Central government, strengthening of, 12–13

Central Hospital at Nanking, 27

Central Planning Board, 72–73, 75

Central Political Committee, 2–3; important changes in, as wartime measure, 4–6

Chiang, Kai-shek, 72; increasing powers of, xvi–xviii; offices held by, xvii–xviii, 6

Childbirth, 34–35

Chin, Yueh-lin, v, vi, vii, xxxvii n., xxxviii–xxxix; biographical sketch of, xv; Education in Contemporary China, 81–99, comments on, xliii–liii

Chinese, dominant racial group in China, 8

Cholera epidemics, 28, 30

Chu, C. K., vi, vii, xxv, xxxii, 36–40; biographical sketch of, xi–xii; The Modern Public Health Movement in China, 26–35, comments on, xxii–xxvi

Chungking government, xvi

Civil war, 12

Class distinctions, 8

Clinics, 34

Coal production, increase in, 69

Commission on Medical Education, 27

Committee of Planning and Examination under each ministry, 72

Communist Party of China, xix and n., xx, 11; position of, xx–xxii

Communists, 10, 11

Competitive entrance examinations at universities, 87

Confucius, xxxvii and n.

Constitutional regime for post-war China, 6, 13, 15

Control Power, 3

County health services, 31

County or *hsien* health centers, 31, 34, 39–40

Credit co-operatives, 66–67

Cressey, G. B., *Geographical Foundations of China*, 46

Dairy products: consumption of, xxv; and problem of nutrition, 22–23

Death rate, 32

Democratic government in China, 15

Diet: of college students, 17; recommendations for, by Nutritional Committee of Chinese Medical Association, 17; minimum standards of, of International Health Committee of League of Nations, 16, 17; of soldiers, 17; of women and children, 18

Diet of China: low animal protein content of, xxiii, 16–18; mineral deficiencies in, 16, 20–21; vitamin deficiency of, xxiii, 16, 18–19; *see also* Nutrition

Diseases: due to mineral deficiencies, 20–21; due to protein deficiency, 17–18; due to vitamin deficiency, 18–19

District Code, new, 13, 14

District Councils, 14–15

Drugs, high price of, xxiii, 44

Economic plans: ten-year, for post-war period, 74; year-by-year, of ministries, 72–74

Economic reconstruction and planning, wartime and post-war, 65–80

Economics, 94–95, 97

Education, xliii; classical, 92; higher, deterioration of, 85–89; intrinsic purpose of, 89–91; for national defense, 91–97; national purpose of, 91–97; planned assaults on, xliv; primary, 83–84; quality of, deterioration of, 83–89; quantity of, increase in, 82–83, 89; secondary, 84

Educational system of China, ancient classical, xlvii n.

Emergency Medical Services Training School, 42, 43

Employment, limited opportunities for, 47, 51

Engineering education, 94–95, 97; importance of sciences and mathematics in, xlviii–lii, 93

Epidemic diseases, 28–30

Epidemics, xxiii

Epidemiological surveys, 31

Examination Power, 3

Executive Yüan, xvii, xviii, 3; overhauling of, 4

Factories: removal of, to inland districts, 68; rural labor in, xxx, xxxv–xxxvi; of wartime United States, lending of, to China, xxxiv–xxxv, 76–77; young people in, xxx, xxxvi, 60–61

Factory production, increase in, 68

Family, influence of, lessening of, xx–xxi

Farm animals, scarcity of, 48

Farm labor: emigration of, due to war, 52–53, 55, 56–57; traditional attitude toward, 49, 57

Farm labor power, surplus, 47, 51

Farm tenancy, 67

Farm wages, low, 47–48, 51

Farmers Bank, 67

INDEX

Farming: experience in, discontinuity of, 57; human labor used in, 48–49; methods, improvement of, xxxi

Farms: of China, average size of, 50, 67; enlargement of, xxx, 67–68

Fei, Hsiao-t'ung, v, vi, vii, xxx, xxxii, xxxiii; biographical sketch of, xiii–xv; Some Social Problems of Free China, 46–64, comments on, xxxv–xliii

Filial prosperity, ideology of, 47, 50, 51

Finance, centralization of, 10

Fishery, and problem of nutrition, 23

Five Power Constitution, 1, 3; developed by Dr. Sun Yat-sen, 2, 6–7

Food: prices of, xxiii–xxiv; increase of supply, xlii–xliii; supply of, xli;

Foodstuffs: of China, adequacy of, 65–66; handling of, and problem of nutrition, 23–24

Free China: backwardness of, in industrialization, 65; self-sufficiency of, in matter of foodstuffs, 65–66

Fung, Yu-lan, "The New Morals," xl–xli

Gasoline production, 68–69

Girls, in factory work, 61

Goiter, 20; incidence of, xxiii

Government: good, desire of Chinese people for, xxi–xxii; of post-war China, 6–7

Government of China, 1–2; comparison of, with that of other countries, xxii; by Kuomintang, 15

Government of Unoccupied China, xv–xxii, 2–15; control of, by Kuomintang, 4

Grant, John B., 26

Hanlin Yüan, xxxix

Harris Institute Round Table discussions, 1943: participants in, v–vii, biographical sketches of, viii–xv; publication of, vii–viii; scope of, iii–v; subjects treated in, vi–vii

Health education, and problem of nutrition, 24–25

Health Section of League of Nations, 38

Health stations, on highway, 31

Hodges, Paul C., vii

Hsien health centers, 31, 34, 39–40

Hull, Cordell, 76

Immunization, 30; in Chinese armies, 41 n.

Income of laborers, increase in, 54, 55

Industrial co-operatives, xxviii–xxix

Industrial and Mining Administration, 69–70

Industrialization of China, xxvi–xxxi, xxxvi, xli–xliii, xlviii, li–lii, 61, 91–97; in hands of government and private enterprise, 69–70; importance of, to United States, 77–80; to meet huge domestic market, 79; as solution to farm problem, 67–68

Infant mortality, xxiii, xxiv, 32

Inflation, 53–54, 62

Institutions of higher learning, number of, 82

Interest rates, xxxiv, 66

International economic co-operation, importance of, 78–80

International Health Committee of League of Nations, 16, 17

Investment of American capital in China, 77–80

Iron production, increase in, 69
Iron and steel plan, 74–75

Japanese aggression in China, 10
Judicial Yüan, 3

"Kiating paralysis," 20–21
Kuomintang, xvi–xxii, 2, 15; in favor of Five Power system, for postwar China, 6; membership in, xix; most powerful party, xviii–xxii; power of, 4

Labor supply, urban, xxix
Landowners, as leisure class, 49
Language of China, basic, 9
Leavens, D. H., vii
Legislative Yüan, 3
Leisure and toil, dichotomy of, 49–50, 51
Leisure class, as dormant labor force, 55–56
Lend-Lease Administration, medical supplies furnished by, 44
Lim, Robert, 42, 43
Linebarger, Paul M. A., xix n., xxvi
Liu, J. Heng, vi, vii, xxv, xxxii; biographical sketch of, xii; as Minister of Health, 26, 36; The Origin and Development of Public Health Service in China, 36–45, comments on, xxii–xxvi
Liu, Nai-chen, v, vi, xxvi, xxxix; biographical sketch of, viii–ix; The Framework of Government in Unoccupied China, 1–15, comments on, xv–xxii

Machinery, lack of, for factories of China, 70
MacNair, H. F., vi
Malaria, 28

Manchus, 8
"Mandarin" language, 9
Mechanization of China, xlviii, lii, 91–97
Medical aids, 41; training schools for, 41–42, 43
Medical officers, junior, 41, 42
Medical personnel of China, shortage of, 32, 40–42
Medical-school students, conscription of, xlv–xlvi
Medical schools in China: equipment of, 43; graduates of, number of, 32, 43; number of, 32, 40, 43
Medical supplies, lack of, xxiv, 43–45
Migration: due to war, 12; of farmers to cities, xxvii, xxix, xxx, xxxv–xxxvi
Military Commission, 3, 4, 5, 6
Milk, powdered, evaporated, and condensed, xxv
Ministries under Executive Yüan, 4
Ministry of Economic Affairs, 69
Ministry of Health, 26, 36, 37, 38
Modernization of China, 93–97
Mohammedans, 8
Monarchy of China, 1
Mongols, 8
Moral code, new, xl–xli
Morality, xxxiii–xxxiv, xl–xli
Mutual Aid Agreement, 76

Nankai University, 86
National army, control of, xxi
National Commission on Aeronautical Affairs, xvii
National Health Administration, 26–33, 38, 43; public health functions of, 27–33
National Institute of Health, 31, 39

INDEX

National Medical and Public Health Authority, 33

National Military Council, xvii

National Resources Commission, 69

National Socialist Party of China, xix–xx

National unity of China, 7, 15; cohesive forces behind, 7–9; disturbing influences affecting, 9–10

Normal Schools, state-service students in, xlvi

Nurses' aids, 41

Nutrition: relationship of, to other factors in Chinese life, 21–25; see also Diet

Nutritional Committee of the Chinese Medical Association, 17

Ogburn, William Fielding, vii

Organic Law of China, revision of 1943 concerning offices held by president, xvii–xviii

Paper production, increase in, 69

Peking Health Demonstration Station, 26, 37

Peking National University, 86–87

Peking Union Medical College, 26; hospital of, 36

People's Political Council, 73–74; appointment to, xx; creation of, by All China Congress, 13; composition of, 14; influence of, upon government, xx; upon public opinion, xx; membership of, 13–14; organization of, xix n.; powers of, 14; representation in, 11

Plague, 28

Planning Commission, 6

Political disturbances in China, causes of, 9–10

Political parties, reconciliation of, 11–12

Political unity of China, 7

Politics of Unoccupied China, xv–xxii

Polygamy, xxxiii

Population of China: density of, 46; uneven distribution of, 46

Population pressure, xxxi–xxxii, xxxv–xxxvi, xli–xliii, 51–52

President of China, powers of, xvii–xviii

Profit rates, xxxiv

Protein deficiency in Chinese diet; see Diet of China

Provincial Health Administration, 33–34

Public administration, three phases of, 72

Public health: of China, xxii–xxiii; movement in China, 26–35

Public Health Personnel Training Institute, 27

Public health services: in China, 30–32; origin and development of, 36–45; types of, 33–34

Purchasing agents in foreign countries, 70

Pure sciences, interest in, xlix–lii, 93

Racial groups in China, 8

Racial minorities, 7–8

Red Cross, Chinese, 27

Regimentation, 97–99

Religious tolerance, 8–9

Reports of ministries, annual, 73–74

Republic of China, 2

Rice producers, purchasing-power of, increase in, 53

Rickets, 18–19, 20

Rural communities: cultural changes in, 55; modernization of, 54

Russell, Bertrand, 81

Scholar: economic status of, xxxvi–xxxvii; position and duties of, xxxvii n., xl; social status of, xxxvi–xxxvii; value of, in marriage market, xxxvii–xxxix

Schools, quality of, lowering of, 83–89

Sciences, teaching of, in connection with engineering, xlix–lii

Scurvy, 19

Security against invasion, 92

Sen, Lin, xvii

Sex distribution of population, xxxiii

Smedley, Agnes, xix n., xxvi

Snow, Edgar, xix n., xxvi

Social classes, mingling of, 54–55

Social medicine, 39

Social problems: caused by redistribution of wealth, 62–63; of Free China, 46–64

Southwest Associated University, 86–87

Spinning industry, increase in, 69

Standards of living: as affected by increase in income, 62–63; in China, improvement of, xxvii–xxviii, xxx–xxxi

State Council, 3; pre-war framework of, unaltered, 3

State medical service, organization of, 33–34

State medicine, xlvi, 33

State-service students, in medical schools, xlvi; in Normal Schools, xlvi

Stein, Guenther, xix n., xxvi

Students: American-returned, xlv; French-returned, xlvii; German-returned, xlv, xlvii; increase in number of, 82–83; number and quality of, xliii–xliv; see also Medical-school students; State-service students

Sun, Yat-sen, xxxiii, 2, 6; The International Development of China, 75–76

Supreme Committee of National Defense, xvii; authority of, over other organs of government, 5–6; organization and powers of, 4–6

Supreme Council of National Defense, xvii, 4, 72; powers of, 5

Tawney, xxxvi, 47

Taxation, 53–54

Teachers: leaving of, to enter factories or government service, 85; quality of, deterioration of, 83, 84

Technological development, blocking of, by cheap labor, 48, 51

Teng, S. Y., vii, xliv, xlvii–xlviii

Tetanus: antitoxin, 41 n.; of newborn, 36–37

Third Party of China, xix n.

Tibetans, 8

Trachoma, 18

Transportation facilities, lack of, as drawback to production, 71

Tsai, Chiao, v, vi, vii, xlvii, xlix, li–lii; biographical sketch of, ix–xi; Problems of Nutrition in Present-Day China, 16–25, comments on, xxii–xxvi

Tsinghua University, 86, 87

Tuberculosis, 18, 29; sanatoriums, 29

Typhus fever, 29

INDEX

Universities: equipment and books of, loss of, 86–87; no military training in, xlv, xlvi; standards of admittance to, lowering of, 88; students in, from occupied territory, 88

Urbanization, xxvii, xxix, xxx, xxxvi

Venereal disease, xxiv; prophylaxis of, 42 n.

Vitamin deficiency in Chinese diet; *see* Diet of China

Water supply, and epidemics, 30

Wealth: attainment of, by illegal means, 51; redistribution of, due to inflation, 62–63; for rural producers, due to war, 53

Wei-Shen-Shu Anti-epidemic Corps, 28–29

West, effect of, on China, 9–10

Western national rivalries, transference of, to Asia, xliv–xlv

World plan, post-war, 98

Wu, Ching-chao, vi, vii, xxxvi, xxxix, xl, xli–xlii, xlv; biographical sketch of, xiii; Economic Reconstruction and Planning: Wartime and Post-war, 65–80, comments on, xxvi–xxxv

Youth: education of, in factories, 60–61; emigration of, from farms, 56–58; prospects of, 59; recruitment of, for factory work, xxx, xxxvi, 60–61

Youth Party of China, xix n., xx

Yuan, Shih-k'ai, 2

Yüans, xvii, xviii, 3; heads and vice-heads of, 5